Sigrid Undset
Chronicler of Norway

Berg Women's Series

Emily Dickinson	DONNA DICKENSON
Elizabeth Gaskell	TESSA BRODETSKY
Mme du Châtelet	ESTHER EHRMAN
Emily Carr	RUTH GOWERS
Simone de Beauvoir	RENEE WINEGARTEN
George Sand	DONNA DICKENSON
Willa Cather	JAMIE AMBROSE
Elizabeth I	SUSAN BASSNETT
Margaret Fuller	DAVID WATSON

In preparation

Rosa Luxemburg	RICHARD ABRAHAM
Edith Wharton	VALERIE SHUBIK
Mme de Sévigné	JEANNE A. AND WILLIAM T. OJALA
Mary Wollstonecraft	JENNIFER LORCH
Dorothy Sayers	MITZI BRUNSDALE

Sigrid Undset,

Chronicler of Norway

Mitzi Brunsdale

BERG *Oxford / New York / Hamburg*

Distributed exclusively in the US and Canada by
St. Martin's Press, New York

Published in 1988 by
Berg Publishers Limited
77 Morrell Avenue, Oxford OX4 1NQ, UK
175 Fifth Avenue/Room 400, New York, NY 10010, USA
Nordalbingerweg 14, 2000 Hamburg 61, FRG

© Mitzi Brunsdale 1988

British Library Cataloguing in Publication Data

Brunsdale, Mitzi
  Sigrid Undset. — (Berg women's series).
  1. Undset, Sigrid — Criticism and interpretation
  I. Title
  839.8′2372   PT8950.U5Z

  ISBN 0–85496–027–9

Library of Congress Cataloging-in-Publication Data

Brunsdale, Mitzi.
  Sigrid Undset/Mitzi Brunsdale.
      p.   cm. — (Berg women's series)
  Bibliography: p.
  Includes index.
  ISBN 0–85496–027–9: $30.00 (U.S.: est.)
  1 Undset, Sigrid, 1882–1949.   2. Authors, Norwegian—20th
century—Biography.   I. Title.   II. Series.
PT8950.U5Z625 1988
839.8′2372—dc19
[B]   87–32660

Printed in Great Britain by Billing & Sons Ltd, Worcester

Contents

1. Two Thousand Years in Norway   1

2. The Longest Years: 1882–1893   18

3. Norwegian Women in Love: 1898–1911   33

4. Poor Humanity: 1911–1919   49

5. The Sins of the Fathers: *Kristin Lavransdatter*, 1919–1924   64

6. Scandinavian Crime and Punishment: *The Master of Hestviken*, 1925–1928   80

7. Catholic Propaganda: 1928–1940   95

8. Meetings and Partings: 1940–1949   112

9. Another Life: Sigrid Undset's Achievements   125

Chronology   133

Bibliographical Notes   150

Index   155

Illustrations

Frontispiece
Sigrid Undset

Between pages 88 and 89
1. Map of Norway
2. Altar, Nidaros Cathedral, Trondheim, Norway
3. Rose Window, Nidaros Cathedral, Trondheim, Norway
4. Nidaros Cathedral (exterior), Trondheim, Norway
5. Karl-Johansgade, Oslo, Norway 1905 — Dissolution of Union with Sweden
6. Bjerkebaek: Sigrid Undset's home at Lillehammer, Norway (official photo # W2863A)
7. Sigrid Undset in Norwegian national dress
8. Sigrid Undset in her middle years
9. Sigrid Undset in old age

Illustrations

For John

'Few better will come after.'

Acknowledgements

I am deeply grateful to Charlotte Blindheim, Curator of the Museum of National Antiquities, University of Oslo, for her gracious assistance and her permission to use material from *Moster Sigrid*; to John Bjørnebye, former Director, and the Norwegian Information Service in the United States, for the use of photographs and other material on Norway and its most celebrated woman writer; to Ivar Havnevik, Chief Editor of H. Aschehoug and Company, for his professional courtesy; to Alfred A. Knopf, Inc., for use of the frontispiece portrait of Sigrid Undset; to my daughters Jean, Maureen and Margaret, for their encouragement; to Betty Karaim, Director, and the Mayville State University Library staff, for their unfailing help; and to Clenora Quanbeck, Marian Tollefsrud, and Orville Bakken, whose insights into the language and the customs of their forefathers have given me an indispensible familiarity with Norwegian life in Sigrid Undset's time. Since I consulted no other persons, any errors in this book are solely my responsibility.

To Aunt Anna and Uncle Joe, and to all my Norwegian-American friends and relatives by marriage who made me welcome, *mange tusend tak*.

M.M.B.

Acknowledgements

I am deeply indebted to [...]

1 Two Thousand Years in Norway

> Very deep is the well of the past.
> Thomas Mann, *Young Joseph and His Brothers*

Sigrid Undset called herself with singular justice 'one who has lived two thousand years in this land'. She would probably have preferred to be known simply as a devoted mother, but before she died in 1949 she had become Norway's foremost woman of letters and one of the world's greatest novelists; a champion of traditional Christian morality; a tireless opponent of totalitarianism; and an analyst of women's issues far beyond her times. Because Sigrid Undset lived out her various roles with uncompromising loyalty to the truth as she saw it, her fiction and essays have the kind of beauty Yeats called 'not natural to an age like this, being high and solitary and most stern', and in these permissive times her work is no longer widely read. In all her writing, especially *Kristin Lavransdatter* and *The Master of Hestviken*,[1] the immense novels of medieval Norway for which she received the Nobel Prize in 1928, Sigrid Undset demonstrated the truth and beauty that can be bought only with human pain, a harsh and noble lesson she learned from Norway's history. Without following that lesson, no understanding of her life and achievement is possible.

Born on 20 May 1882, Sigrid Undset was a precocious child who grew up in the liberal atmosphere of a Norway reawakening to its national consciousness, and very early she began to share her archaeologist father's devotion to Scandinavian antiquity. Once the homeland of savagely individualistic Vikings who were the scourge of Europe from the mid-800s to the beginning of the twelfth century, Norway had been ruled since 1397 by outsiders, first Danes, then Swedes. In the 1880s Norway's consuming interest in its past accompanied its struggle for independence which culminated in 1905, and when Sigrid Undset was a little girl, her country was seeking a national identity in its history, its folk tales and ballads, and its *landsmål* (native form of the language) known as *nynorsk*, the language of Norwegian valleys

1

Danish influence. At the same time, the religious scepticism then flourishing in Scandinavia moved Sigrid Undset's mother to attempt to instil rationalistic views in her children, but Sigrid Undset seemed to rebel against them, and her growing opposition to *fin-de-siècle* pragmatism and materialism eventually paralleled her acceptance of Roman Catholic dogma.

Just as Norway was turning to its past for inspiration at this critical point in its national development, Sigrid Undset immersed herself in medieval Norwegian history during her ten years at an office job in Oslo. The old myths, legends and sagas became as familiar to her as her own family's tales, and she became as comfortable in the Middle Ages as she was in the Scandinavia of her own time.

In 1913, Norway became the first European country to extend full voting rights to women. The young heroines of Sigrid Undset's early fiction found their desire for independence at grave odds with their yearning for love and marriage, a problem still bedevilling women today. After writing several modern stories centred on that conflict, Sigrid Undset at last confronted it in the medieval setting of *Kristin Lavransdatter* and by doing so she found a master that she could declare her Lord. Her conversion in 1924 marked her adoption of Roman Catholic ethics as the answer both to her own spiritual quest and to the devastation of European culture after the First World War, a civilisation-wide echo of the moral vacuum she felt that the twentieth century had become. In her next novel, Sigrid Undset used her hero, Olav Audunsson, the master of Hestviken, to affirm her belief that man must atone for his sins. Olav's spiritual journey symbolises the idea that Roman Catholicism is the sole means by which man can reach salvation, finally overcoming the Old Norse sense of individual honour. Like that of her contemporary brothers in the faith, Paul Claudel and Jacques Maritain, Sigrid Undset's religious bias threatened to overwhelm her psychological insight and her widely praised literary talent. Just before the Second World War, however, she seemed to be recovering a balanced historical realism with *Madame Dorthea*, her last novel, which the Nazi invasion of Norway prevented her from completing.

As a child, Sigrid Undset had exhibited an unusual gift for observing the world around her and the actions and even the motives of the people she met. Her analytic power grew throughout her life, and her essays, articles and speeches all reveal a keen grasp of contemporary events. She paid a heavy price for raising one of the earliest objections to Hitler's Third Reich; her eldest son was killed in Norway's 62-day resistance, and she was forced into exile in the USA, where her grief and a heavy load of wartime activities brought her career as a creative artist to a close. To the end, Sigrid Undset upheld the ideals of Christian humanism, and she continually insisted that her immersion in Norway's past had strongly implanted them in her soul. Already in 1919 she had observed: 'I think the reason why I understand our own time so well, or see it so clearly, is because ever since I was a child I had some kind of living memories from an earlier age to compare with it'.[2]

Sigrid Undset's Norway is a ruggedly beautiful and inhospitable land. Nearly three-quarters of its 125,000 square miles is mountainous and almost a quarter remains forested. Only 4 per cent of its total area, slightly less than three times the size of England, is arable, and so despite the temperate Gulf Stream climate which keeps the deep fjords ice-free even in the long Northern winters, Norwegians have always set a high value on farmland that would yield a decent living. Evidence from the Stone Age indicates that hunters and fishermen inhabited Norway's coast from about 8,000 BC, probably worshipping a protective deity identifiable with the thunder-god later called Thor, and by 3,000 BC, Norway's interior was settled and agriculture was beginning to develop. Bronze Age burial mounds dating from 1,300 to 500 BC testify to Norway's growing social organisation and the worship of additional gods, the twin Germanic fertility deities Freyr and Freyja. Their cult of peace and plenty differs strongly from the battle cult of Odin, known in other Germanic lands as Wotan or Woden, the mystical All-Father of warriors and Lord of the Slain, god of poets and magic, whose worship entered Scandinavia in the Iron Age, the first centuries after Christ, when Germanic tribes swept across Europe bringing a justice of the sword the world has not yet forgotten.

As the Roman Empire crumbled in the fourth and fifth centuries, stories of historic Germanic kings like Theodoric of the Ostrogoths, Gundiharius of the Burgundians and the fearsome Attila the Hun became intertwined with legendary figures like Sigurd the Dragon-Slayer and Brynhild, the lover he fatally rejected. Around AD 600 the historical chieftain Arthur of legendary fame vainly mustered British tribes against Anglo-Saxon invaders; the cultural fusion of pagan Germanic and Christian elements which ensued is evident in the Old English epic *Beowulf*. At the same time, Norway was evolving into a land of twenty-nine *fylker*, each under its own king, who often served as the priest of his district, reading omens, propitiating its gods, and maintaining its pagan temple. Not content with preying on one another, Scandinavian warriors began taking to their deadly longships in the eighth century, harrying Ireland, Britain, and Europe and enriching their lairs on the fjords with slaves and booty. From the ninth to the eleventh century Northern warrior-poets called skalds celebrated Viking exploits and the myths that inspired them in highly complex oral poetry, said to be a gift from Odin, like the runic alphabet used in magical lore.

Time and the absence of contemporary written texts have obscured Viking religious practices, derived from beliefs of the Proto-Germanic Indo-European culture which had divided into Eastern (Gothic), Western (North German and English), and Northern (Scandinavian) branches by the fourth century AD. Most present-day knowledge of Germanic religion comes from Tacitus' *Germania*, c. AD 100, and from the *Elder Edda* and *Younger Edda*, composed orally in the ninth century and drawn from much earlier material, and written down in the thirteenth century, as well as from archaeological evidence of Viking artefacts scattered from North America to Byzantium. The old religion stubbornly persisted in Scandinavia; conversion of the European Germanic tribes began in the fourth century, and in 597 Aethelbert became the first Christian king of Anglo-Saxon England, but Norwegians carried on pagan customs for at least 200 years after Olaf Tryggvasson, Norway's first Christian king, died in 1000. Descendants of the Vikings continue to toast one another with '*Skol!*' (Skull!), claiming implicitly, '. . . we Scandinavians still have one foot in Odin's realm, and when we drink a toast we mean something quite serious'.[3]

One certainty dominated Old Norse belief: fate, to which the gods themselves must bow, ruled their universe, and since destruction was inevitable, all that mattered was the courage with which men and women met their deaths, winning the only eternal life they knew, the immortality only a skald could give. At the centre of the Old Norse universe was the mighty tree Yggdrasil, linking the underworld of the giants and the dead to the Middle Earth of men and to lofty Asgard, home of the gods. In its roots lived the Norns, female guardians of fate, who watered the tree from the Well of Mimir, source of all wisdom; but not far away lurked the giants, only temporarily held at bay by the gods, and evil monsters constantly gnawed at Yggdrasil's roots. On a day called Ragnarok, it was prophesied, the traitor god Loki, the grey wolf Fenris, and the ancient serpent coiled around the earth in the depths of the sea would attack Asgard, and both gods and men would perish; an age of peace would dawn, and a man and a woman would repopulate a new earth regenerated by the flaming destruction of the old.

The religious lore contained in the *Eddas* and the later sagas yields indispensable insights into the Norwegian character and Sigrid Undset's depiction of it. In one of the oldest Norse legends, the warlike gods of the Aesir, lords of magic and the lightning, vanquished the gentler Vanir, fertility deities, and absorbed them into the Aesir pantheon. Many historians believe the myth records the clash between Northern Europes megalithic agricultural peoples and the Indo-European invaders of the Battle Axe, while structuralists like Georges Dumézil see the Aesir and the Vanir as 'two complementary terms in a religious and ideological structure', a myth *'older* [Dumézil's italics] than the Germanic peoples', that preserves 'the complex elements and nuances of a "lesson" on the structure of Indo-European societies'. Thor, Freyr and Odin form a tripartite theological structure that 'sums up the needs and imaginations of men'[4] and dominates the mythology of the North.

First among the Aesir, though not the oldest or most revered god of the ancient Norsemen, was Odin, lord of hosts, whose cult was dominant in Denmark. In Norway, only the princely warriors followed Odin; as the Christian historian Saxo Grammaticus claimed in *Gesta Danorum*: '. . . the perilous deeds which chiefs attempt are not to be done by the ventures of common men' (quoted in Dumézil, *Gods of the Ancient Northmen*, p. 78). In the *Hávamál*, a poem of the *Elder Edda*, Odin describes how he won wisdom by being pierced by a sword and being hanged on a tree, a grim precedent for the sacrifices Norsemen felt essential to victory in battle. According to one legend, Odin won the gift of poetic inspiration for himself and his followers from the spring of Mimir; according to another, poetry rose from the blood of Kvasir, whose name derives from *kvas*, still the word used in Jutland for crushed fruit. The Aesir and Vanir had created Kvasir with their saliva, a primitive form of fermentation, to celebrate their truce, a victory of the gods of magic over the gods of fertility; but intoxication, whether it comes from drink or poetry, can betray as well as bless. Many ancient texts as well as Sigrid Undset's novels reveal the Norsemen's deep distrust of the forces they once called by the name of Odin, who was also the trickster god of the dead.

The Aesir thunder-god Thor retained the spiritual allegiance of the Norsemen longest. They loved him best, the happy god of oaths and the mighty hammer, because he defended the stability of the civilisation they had built in defiance of their inimical environment and their neighbours' greed. It was not the warrior aristocracy but men of hard work and goodwill who dedicated the sacred pillars of their judgement seats and homes to Thor. In him were embodied their most basic laws, the keeping of faith and the necessity for individual vengeance. Thor's worship lasted longest of all the gods, from Norway's dim prehistory well past the days of Olaf Tryggvasson, when Norwegian Christians and heathens alike considered 'the god of the land' Christ's chief adversary because, paradoxically, his worship came closest to Christianity; in the Norse imagination, Thor's hammer, after all, was not so far in shape and meaning from the cross of Christ.

Not so widely worshipped in western Scandinavia as Odin and Thor, but none the less representing the most elemental human drives, were the Vanir god Freyr and his female counterpart Freyja. Women in the sacred act of childbirth cried out to Freyja, the only maternal figure in the Asgard of the *Eddas*. Her special gift was divination, a manifestation of the imputed connection with the supernatural for which Germanic tribes prized their women highly. The primitive fertility goddess eternally mourns her consort who dies to renew his land, relinquishing it to a virile young successor whom the goddess helps bring to light, the paradigm of human generations. The ancient Swedes loved Freyr so well they sent their early kings down to violent death in his mythical footsteps to assure their crops. Similarly, since Norwegians believed Freyr (Yng) had founded the Uppsala dynasty of the Ynglings, they divided the corpse of the ninth-century Yngling ruler Halfdan the Black among the four districts of Vestfold, his kingdom in south-east Norway. Their devotion bore important fruit; Halfdan's son Harold Fairhair became the first king of a united Norway in 872.

British archaeologist Hilda Ellis Davidson has remarked: 'The solutions [to human problems] offered by the great gods — temporary forgetfulness from Odin, belief in rebirth and continuation of the family from Freyr, protective strength and a sense of order provided by Thor — were not in themselves sufficient to silence the threat of the dragon and the monsters'.[5] The Norse gods yielded to the relentless law of mortality, leaving unforgettable stories of their heroic ideal, the doomed battle in a narrow place against overwhelming odds, in the literature of the North and in the hearts of many of their descendants. Even today the Orkney poet George Mackay Brown celebrates the Vikings' 'laughter and a deep enjoyment of life, believing it was better to go into the darkness young and strong than to die "a straw death"'.[6]

That kind of courage has reverberated throughout the realistic tradition of Scandinavian literature. The Old Norse myths squarely face the darkest mysteries of man's being and his greatest terror, the mind's disintegration in madness or death. From the *Eddas* and the sagas to the psychological realism of Ibsen, Strindberg, Hamsun, Lagerkvist and Sigrid Undset, Scandinavian literature has unflinchingly probed the deeps of the human unconscious where the most profound human urges originate.

As ancient as the myths which D.H. Lawrence claimed treat matters that go too deep in the blood and soul for rational analysis and as modern as the pressures modern psychiatry is only beginning to plumb, the Scandinavian realistic tradition in which Sigrid Undset made herself a distinguished place rests on the lessons of living taught in the Old Norse heritage. Hilda Ellis Davidson remarks that these myths reveal no bitterness at life's unfairness, but rather celebrate heroic resignation: '. . . courage, adventure, and the wonders of life are matters for thankfulness. . . . The great gifts of the gods were readiness to face the world as it was, the luck that sustains men in tight places, and the opportunity to win that glory which alone can outlive death' (Davidson, *Gods and Myths*, p. 218). Sigrid Undset, in her *Saga of Saints*, called the Viking Age 'a love poem to a God who remained hidden', reconciling Norway's pagan history with the passion that brought her to her own religious faith.

A remarkable cultural and political phenomenon followed Harold Fairhair's unification of Norway in 872. To crush the power of rival lords, Harold had revoked the right of Norwegian farmers to own their hereditary lands, and outraged emigrants flocked to virgin Iceland. Many cast the sacred house-pillars of their abandoned Norwegian homes adrift from their longships and followed Thor's choice to new homes on the Icelandic coast. By 930 when the settlement of Iceland was virtually complete, Iceland's foremost *gothar*, warrior priests, gathered each June at Thingvellir for the Althing, the elected Icelandic General Assembly, which provided legislative and judicial authority for the nation and created its vital cultural centre.

Because the Althing lacked executive capacity for its legislative decisions, crimes had to be punished by personal, not governmental, retribution. Icelandic might increasingly became right, eventually leading to annexation by Norway in 1262, but at the same time Icelandic skalds dominated Norwegian culture. Iceland's oral poetic tradition descended from Old Germanic epic verse, a rhythmic alliterative form convenient to memorise and declaim, that kept alive the lore of the great Germanic Iron Age migrations, like the tale of Sigurd and Brynhild woven into the Icelandic *Volsungasaga*. Anonymous traditional verse of the Viking Age was more popular with the humble folk, but in their more sophisticated compositions the warrior-skalds sang their chieftain's deeds to ensure his immortality and their own, Odin's ambivalent gift to man. Harald Beyer has observed that farmers have little place in this poetry: 'Its heroes live on the tragic plane . . . [in] two contrasting types, the man of good fortune and the man of shadows. The first is the skald, who is brave and openhearted, boldly seeking the joys of life; but the latter is the medicine man, the mystic who feels himself to be in the grasp of evil powers'.[7]

Icelandic skalds adorned Norway's royal courts from the time of Harold Fairhair to the fourteenth century. Before he died, Harold redivided his kingdom among his twenty sons, making one of them Overking. This was Erik Bloodaxe, who ruled from 930 to 934. Harold thus set in motion the savage internecine struggle for the throne that accompanied Christianity's painful introduction to Norway. Both Erik and his successor, Haakon the Good, who was raised at the Christian court of Aethelstan of England, were baptised, but they surrendered the new faith in the face of powerful opposition from their pagan countrymen. Erik's skald, Egil Skalla-Grimsson, kept Erik's memory as a pagan king alive in a resounding memorial ode, and Earl Haakon Sigurds-son, who ruled as Norway's last pagan king from 970 to 995, gathered skalds around him, giving their art 'its last pagan renaissance' (Beyer, *A History*, p. 39). Olaf Tryggvasson, 995–1000, whom historian Gwyn Jones describes as 'Christ's best hatchet-man',[8] founded Norway's holy capital Nidaros, now Trondheim, in 997, but skalds found increasing difficulty in adapting their poetry, whose roots and sombre images stemmed from the fatalistic Old Norse mythology, to the new faith that promised resurrection.

In the reign of St Olaf, 1016–29, who was himself a gifted poet, the Latin alphabet taught by missionary monks began to supersede the Norse *futhark*, runes used principally in magical inscriptions. Olaf saved the skalds from relinquishing their art completely by stressing their role as historians and shapers of opinion; at Stiklestad, his last battle, Olaf set his skalds within the innermost circle of his warriors, saying to them, one recalled: '. . . you shall be here and see the events that occur, so that you can tell about them and make poems about them later on' (quoted in ibid., p. 40). Olaf's close friend the Icelandic skald Sigvat Thórdarson convinced Olaf's son Magnus, known later as 'the Good', not to take vengeance for his father's death, an unusual example of cheek-turning that must have contributed more to the establishment of Christian ethics in Norway than most of the sermons on loving kindness given by imported priests.

During the eleventh and twelfth centuries, the skalds increasingly used Christian themes, but skaldic art continued to decline. Written, not oral composition, became fashionable, and the skald's demanding metrical forms gave way to prose sagas, although as late as the reign of Erik Magnusson, 1280–99, poets resided at the Norwegian court.

Norway's Age of Sagas, from the mid-twelfth to the end of the thirteenth century, marks the zenith of her medieval history and provides the settings of Sigrid Undset's two greatest novels. The

9

royal line founded by Harold Fairhair faltered in the early 1100s while the power of the Norwegian Church burgeoned, directed by Nicholas Breakspear, who established Nidaros as his archepiscopal see and later claimed the papacy as Adrian IV (1154–9), the only English pope, as a reward for the success of his Norwegian mission. Manoeuvrings among rival claimants to Norway's throne allowed a later archbishop to accept the country as a fief of the Church in 1164 as his condition for crowning Magnus V. During Magnus' twenty-year reign, continual uprisings shook the throne, as the *Birkebeiner* (Birch-legs), small landowners who distrusted the growing influence of the Church, battled with the aristocratic *Bagler* (Crozier-men), who supported the bishops' heavy temporal claims. Magnus died at the Battle of Nordnes in 1184 despite the support of the Danes, the Norwegian Church, and the old aristocracy, and from 1184 to 1202 the *Birkebeiner* King Sverre founded a new commerce-based nobility, defying the Archbishop of Nidaros, who from Denmark laid all of Norway under interdict. During the brief reign of Inge II, placed in power by the Church, the *Birkebeiner* secretly raised Sverre's grandson Haakon the Lame and later set him on the Norwegian throne, overcoming the rival claims of Inge's brother Earl Skule, who had acted as Haakon's regent from 1217 to 1223. Skule rebelled in 1240 and was killed by the *Birkebeiner*, and Pope Innocent reluctantly but formally recognised Haakon as Norway's king, ushering in the nation's first period of peace and prosperity, during which Sigrid Undset's history of *The Master of Hestviken* takes place. Before Haakon fell in the Battle of Largs in 1263 attempting to conquer Scotland through the Orkneys, his splendid court had witnessed the acquisition of Iceland and Greenland, important legal reforms that paved the way for an entirely new judicial code under Haakon's son Magnus Law-mender, and an unprecedented flowering of Old Norse literature.

King Haakon preferred the courtly romances then sweeping Europe to the historical sagas of Norwegian kings based on church chronicles and written from 1170 to 1250, and to the family sagas, begun as early as 1200 as briefer episodic narratives of Icelandic feuds during the tenth and early eleventh centuries. Haakon commissioned the translation of Thomas of Britain's *Tristan and Iseut*, which became Norway's most popular 'lying saga', the Norsemen's name for literature intended primarily as entertainment, usually dealing with the period prior to the time of Harold Fairhair or the even more ancient past.

The leading figure of medieval Scandinavian literature was Snorri Sturluson, a powerful Icelandic aristocrat and friend of Earl Skule, who favoured the old skaldic warrior tradition. Snorri became entangled in Norwegian schemes to annex Iceland, and for taking Skule's part against King Haakon, royal assassins slew Snorri in his home on 22 September 1141. Snorri's *Heimskringla*, Sigrid Undset's model for her *Saga of Saints*, surveys Norway's history to 1177 through the royal succession, combining historical information with traditional legend. Snorri's masterpiece is the *Prose Edda*, *c.* 1222, an account of Old Norse myth and an attempt to revive skaldic art with a treatise on poetic diction and metrics.

Snorri's historical insight contributed to the development of the anonymous Icelandic family sagas written towards the end of the twelfth century. Thirty are extant, long historical novels based on real events but including elements of chivalric and heroic adventure, 'all of them marked', Harald Beyer observes, 'by a consciously artistic intention of psychologically characterising the personalities described' (Beyer, *A History*, p. 53). The saga style resembles a snow-covered volcano, cold and calm on the surface, its depths glowing with passion; these sober, understated narratives achieve powerful psychological realism through characterisations, which many scholars agree are 'more complex and subtle than could be accommodated in the viking [sic] morality of the Eddic poems' (ibid., p. 53).

The most famous and best loved of the family sagas in ancient as well as modern times, *Njal's Saga*,[9] presents figures acting out of a bewildering range of motives from coldest revenge to most fervent loyalty. The wise Christian father Njal comforts, sacrifices and mediates, to maintain a friendship as long as human patience can endure; while his eldest son, the magnetic pale Skarphedin, whose smile, like Brynhild's, inspires more terror than ever *berserker* fury can, brings fate crashing down upon them all. Skarphedin, a man of shadows and Odin's chosen warrior, fascinated Sigrid Undset even at eleven years old, when she first read the *Njal's Saga* in her grandfather's library at Trondheim — the turning-point, she later maintained, of her entire life.

From 1263 to 1280, Magnus VI irreversibly changed life in

Norway. Magnus ended the costly war with Scotland by ceding the Hebrides and the Isle of Man to Alexander III for a large sum. Norway, whose Church had called a halt to Viking raids, no longer needed these islands. Magnus' most far-reaching innovation was a new legal code that covered all four districts of Norway alike, and for the first time made the Norwegian throne the chief source of justice. By repealing the old *wergild* laws which dictated personal vengeance, Magnus instituted the concept of crime as an offence against the state, not the individual, significantly limiting the landowners' need to support private militias for revenge or enterprise and not incidentally protecting Magnus himself from possible overthrow. New municipal laws gave Norwegian cities freedom from rural control, and by choosing his own ruling council and introducing European customs and titles for them, Magnus founded a new governing class that the once-haughty *lendermaend*, Norway's hereditary lords, could not shake. By securing a limitation of the Church's powers, Magnus made the *lendermaend* politically impotent by 1280.

By the time saga writing ceased in 1300, Magnus' son Haakon V, who ruled from 1299 to 1319, had paralysed the *lendermaend* completely. The ancient warrior caste was dying; they had spent themselves against the *Birkebeiner* and declined in prestige under Magnus' legal code, and in the early years of the fourteenth century Norway's deepening impoverishment told most heavily upon them. The *lendermaend* had gained their wealth and power from several sources: from Viking raids, now outlawed by the Church; from slave labour, abolished by Magnus Law-mender; from European commerce, now monopolised by the North German Hanseatic League; and from the once-rich fur trade, into which the Russians were making serious incursions. The popular thirteenth-century ballads in which the nobility celebrated their ancient ideals passed in the fourteenth century to the common folk, who linked the ballad form with the prose *eventyr*, consciously imaginative fairy tales, and *sagn*, stories with realistic and localised details. Such stories lightened the lot of farmers and labourers struggling with the grinding poverty that had overtaken Norway, exacerbated by the uncertainties of international power struggles. Norway's King Magnus VII, son of Haakon's daughter Ingeborg and Duke Erik of Sweden, ruled both countries from 1319 to 1343, and into this complicated arena of shifting political and cultural cross-currents, a time 'singularly poor in living historical records'[10] and ravaged by the cataclysmic Black Death, Sigrid Undset placed her most famous novel, *Kristin Lavransdatter*.

Probably no country could have maintained its independence under such conditions. In 1397, lacking a Norwegian heir, Erik of Pomerania was crowned King of Denmark, Sweden, and Norway in a Union 'never to be dissolved'. Norway sank to the level of a Danish province during the Protestant Reformation, and by 1539 Danish pastors were even appointed to Norwegian Lutheran parishes. Although Norway's peasantry remained free while Danish peasants were serfs, Norway continued to pay the price for Danish aggression until 1814, when without Norwegian consent Denmark's Frederick VI ceded Norway to Sweden in the Treaty of Kiel.

From the birth of Norway's National Movement in the early nineteenth century, Norwegian politics went hand in hand with literature. Norwegians objected to the Treaty of Kiel on the grounds that disposing of an entire kingdom without its people's consent violated international law, and on 17 May (*Syttende Mai*) 1814 they declared their independence by adopting a Constitution based on those of the USA, France and Spain, creating a single-chamber National Assembly, the Storthing, which the King cannot veto or dissolve. After two weeks of hostilities, Norway accepted the King of Sweden on the condition that the Norwegian Constitution be retained, and in the Act of Union which the two governments ratified the following year, Sweden and Norway maintained a military alliance under Carl XIV, while retaining individual governments, parliaments, armies, navies and customs.

A fundamental difference in their concepts of union separated the two countries, however, since Norway's Constitution abolished its hereditary nobility in 1818, paving the way for its peasantry to become the ruling class. Swedes, on the other hand, widely and erroneously considered Norway one of their western provinces, and the absolutist Swedish monarchs defied Norway's 'Peasant Storthings', which, beginning in 1833, called for increased governmental economy. The resulting tensions were fuelled by the political–literary controversy between the republican poet Henrik Wergeland, a zealous proponent of Norway's national characteristics, who favoured full equality with Sweden, and Johan Sebastian Welhaven, a famous conservative supporting Norway's literary ties with Denmark, whose language Norwegians had come to share almost completely.

Around 1830, Norway, like Denmark and Germany, experienced an awakening of interest in the literature and art of its people, a desire 'to fill the gaps in Norwegian cultural history, to cement the bond between the old and new Norway' (Beyer, 'Sigrid Undset', p. 141). The Asbjørnson–Moe 'Norwegian Folk Tales' (*Norske Folkeeventyr*) of 1841–4 retold the old *eventyr* in a style as close to oral narrative as possible, laying the groundwork for a new Norwegian prose style,[11] and genuine medieval ballads and folk music appeared for the first time in M.B. Landsted's 1852–3 collection, 'Norwegian Ballads' (*Norske Folkevisor*), strongly influencing young Ibsen, who based his early dramas heavily on folk themes. At the same time, the Norwegian linguist Ivar Aasen wanted to abandon the Dano–Norwegian *riksmål* (*bokmål*) for a new written language, its *landsmål* (native form) known as *nynorsk*, deriving from the connection Aasen demonstrated in 1848 between western Norwegian dialects and the Old Norse of the sagas. Other scholars, like Knud Knudsen, preferred to introduce dialect and colloquialisms into the Dano–Norwegian language. In Sigrid Undset's time, the *riksmål–landsmål* question was as unsettled as it remains today.

Norway's National Romanticism lasted only from about 1845 to 1850, yielding to a new spirit of realism which by the close of the century brought the great Norwegian dramatists Ibsen and Bjørnson worldwide renown. Great Britain's abolition of the Navigation Acts in 1830 spurred the growth of the Norwegian merchant fleet, and Norway's increasing industrialisation supplied concrete proof of growing materialistic and pragmatic trends becoming evident in philosophy and literature. Buttressed by Darwinism, new views of man as a product, if not a victim, of his heredity and his environment were becoming popular, especially in Bjørnson's positivism, which saw man's chief duty as improvement of his lot on earth, since metaphysical matters were considered beyond human grasp. Other Norwegian writers turned to contemporary social issues like the labour movement, women's rights, and education, approaching a Zolaesque naturalistic emphasis on the dismal aspects of life.

Norway's two best-known nineteenth-century women writers, Camilla Collett and Amalie Skram, both treated women's positions at home and in society with a frankness unusual for their time. Collett, Henrik Wergeland's sister, produced Norway's first novel of social purpose, *The Governor's Daughters*, 1854–5, which she called 'a shriek', a passionate demand for understanding that women need — and deserve — more from life than socially acceptable marriages. Harald Beyer notes that 'Camilla Collett had stirred up discussion, but Amalie Skram caused consternation' (ibid., p. 239). Skram's pessimistic novels of the 1880s revealed poverty as the cause of human sin, whose wages, she insisted, could only be death. Her insight into the plight of women and children trapped in minutely observed economic, social, and hereditary pressures is lightened 'with a sympathy that elevates the spirit and gives a deeper understanding' (ibid., p. 239).

As Norway's realistic literature came to dominate Scandinavia in the latter half of the nineteenth century, difficulties with Sweden increased. From 1859, the Swedes had been pressing for the establishment of a common parliament, with two Swedish representatives to each Norwegian. The Norwegian Storthing resoundingly defeated the revised Act of Union in 1871 through a coalition of the 'lawyers' party' led by Johan Sverdrup and the 'peasant party' of Soren Jaaboek. This alliance founded the Norwegian Venstre ('Left' or Liberal) Party, which soon became a powerful force in Norwegian politics.

When Norwegians celebrated their thousand years as a kingdom in 1873, Sverdrup called for governmental ministers to be admitted to the Storthing and take part in its proceedings, a reform the Swedish King Carl XV resisted as a threatened introduction of full parliamentary government. Carl's successor Oscar II wrestled with the Storthing and its president Sverdrup until 1882, the year of Sigrid Undset's birth, when Sverdrup and Bjørnson engineered a mammoth Liberal victory that brought on a two-year government crisis. At last in June, 1884, the Storthing's demands forced the Swedish king to ask Sverdrup to form a Norwegian government, and over the next two decades, while Sigrid Undset was growing up, Liberal reforms led to Norway's full independence in 1905. Norwegians chose the second son of King Frederick VIII of Denmark as Haakon VII and crowned him in the eleventh-century Trondheim Cathedral, a demonstration of Norway's unbreakable link with its ancient past.

That same cathedral looms above all of Sigrid Undset's novels like the first Old Norse prayer in stone, 'the grandest proof our history can offer', her friend and mentor Fredrik Paasche wrote, 'of the power which lay in the longing to overcome isolation and poverty'.[12] Like the stubborn old master builders at Nidaros who used stone in Norway for the first time, drawing on Norman, Romanesque, and English Gothic styles, Sigrid Undset battled with her environment to shape diverse materials into an unquestionably Norwegian art. She drew from the Old Norse myths, the backbone of Norway's culture and the well-spring of many Norwegian national characteristics; she immersed herself in the sagas, whose understatement heightens the burning creative tension between pagan and Christian ideals; she loved Norway's folklore and ballads as much as she cherished the flowers of its majestic countryside, and she incorporated them all into her fiction. She sympathised with women's lot because she came to know it all too well herself, and she staunchly defended Norway's right to independence even though she rejected the materialism inherent in its liberal political orientation. Sigrid Undset sought many paths, ancient and modern, in her pursuit of the truths in which her life and work were rooted.

Notes

1. See 'Bibliographical Notes'. *Kristin Lavransdatter* is cited from the Bantam paperback edition; *The Master of Hestviken*, from the New American Library Plume paperback edition.
2. From a letter Sigrid Undset wrote in 1919 to Nini Roll Anker, quoted in Carl Bayerschmidt, *Sigrid Undset* (New York: Twayne, 1970), p. 38. This study is cited hereafter in the text.
3. Robertson Davies, *World of Wonders* (Harmondsworth and New York: Penguin, 1975), p. 86.
4. Georges Dumézil, *Gods of the Ancient Northmen*, Einar Haugen (ed.), trans. C. Scot Littleton et al. (Berkeley, California: University of California Press, 1973), pp. 4, 12.
5. Hilda R. Ellis Davidson, *Gods and Myths of Northern Europe* (Har-

mondsworth and New York: Penguin, 1964), p. 162. This work is cited hereafter in the text.

6. George Mackay Brown, *A Time to Keep and Other Stories* (New York: Vanguard, 1987), p. iv.

7. Harald Beyer, 'Sigrid Undset', in Einar Haugen (ed.), *A History of Norwegian Literature*, trans. Einar Haugen (New York: New York University Press, 1956), pp. 10–12. This work is cited hereafter in the text.

8. Gwyn Jones, *A History of the Vikings* (Oxford and New York: Oxford University Press, 1968), p. 135.

9. The title is also translated as *The Saga of Burnt Njal*, or simply the *Njála*. See *Njal's Saga*, trans. Carl F. Bayerschmidt and Lee M. Hollander (London: Allen and Unwin, 1955).

10. Alrik Gustafson, 'Christian Ethics in a Pagan World', in *Six Scandinavian Novelists* (Minneapolis, Minn.: University of Minnesota Press, 1968), p. 31.

11. Peter Christen Asbjørnsen and Moltke Moe, *Norske Folkeeventyr*, 2 vols. 1841–4; trans. as *Popular Tales from the Norse* (Edinburgh, 1858), and by Sigrid Undset as *True and Untrue and Other Norse Tales* (New York: Knopf, 1945).

12. Quoted from Fredrik Paasche in A.H. Wisnes, *Sigrid Undset: A Study in Christian Realism*, trans. P.G. Foote (New York: Sheed and Ward, 1953), p. 100.

2 The Longest Years: 1882–1893

> Never trust the artist: trust the tale.
> D.H. Lawrence, 'Why the Novel Matters'

In most of her photographs and public statements, Sigrid Undset turned an austere, even stern, face to her public. Her essential shyness made her seem cool and often reserved, but despite her reticence about her private life she recorded invaluable glimpses of her childhood in *The Longest Years*,[1] 1934, a fictionalised biography tracing the eleven years between her birth and her father's death in 1893. Written in her early fifties, when her established style and rigorous honesty reinforced the acute observations she had made as a child, *The Longest Years* illuminates both her mature artistry and her first steps towards it.

A sophisticated pattern, one that Sigrid Undset must have deliberately chosen, underlies the deceptively simple surface of *The Longest Years*. Because of her father's declining health, the family moved several times to increasingly humble surroundings; her outlook naturally widened and her perceptions sharpened into subtlety, but the stages of psychological growth that Sigrid Undset chose to highlight more than forty years later mirror the cultural and spiritual development of Norway itself, the fountainhead of her art. As it was with her country, so too were Sigrid Undset's most profound experiences touched by grief.

Sigrid Undset's father Ingvald came from the stubborn and religious peasant stock of Østerdal near Trondheim, and to the end of his life he considered himself a man of Trøndelag. As boys he and his friend Henrik Mathiesen, later a noted historian, spent hours exploring the Trondheim cathedral; Mathiesen recalled that Ingvald Undset was one of those fortunate souls '. . . who, when the hour comes, are never for a moment in doubt as to what work they will dedicate themselves to'.[3] Ingvald Undset's vocation was Norway's past. In 1871, the year of Heinrich Schliemann's excavations at Hissarlik, the site of ancient Troy, Undset brought his studies at the Trondheim Cathedral School to a brilliant end and began a career in archaeology, a field then breaking the boundaries of knowledge. He met Anne Charlotte Gyth, the talented daughter of a prominent Danish attorney and chancery councillor, while he was studying for his doctorate at the University in Copenhagen. Not long after their marriage in 1881 he went down with a serious case of malaria while on a Mediterranean research trip, and they had to return to Charlotte's family home at Kalundborg, Denmark, where Sigrid, their eldest daughter, was born in 1882. She remarked in 1940: 'As I was the baby that upset their plans I suppose I was what you would call an unwanted child. Perhaps that was why I became an awfully spoilt child afterwards'.[3]

The previous year, his study *The Beginnings of the Iron Age in Northern Europe* had won Ingvald Undset the impressive international scholarly reputation he was to enjoy for so short a time. His daughter recalled in *The Longest Years* how her Trøndelag grandfather's pride in his son overcame 'that ineradicable feeling about "foreign parts"' that many Norwegians possess; she saw that '[one] could foster as deep a suspicion as one wished about everything in "the great world" outside — all the same, praise and fame from abroad were nearly the greatest a Norwegian could achieve' (quoted in Winsnes, *Sigrid Undset*, p. 11).

Sigrid Undset also knew that her mother delighted in sharing research and travel with a man who loved her so deeply. As seen in *The Longest Years*, however, Charlotte Undset seems to have had the kind of intelligence that can appear to a woman to be more a curse than a blessing when she is just learning to be a mother, especially since daughters are generally readier to pounce on real or imagined maternal faults than to appreciate virtues which life has not yet equipped them to understand. Gifted women like Charlotte Undset, unable by circumstance to exercise their own considerable talents except vicariously through their husband's careers, suffer from an intellectual deprivation far more severe than any bodily hunger. Already an outsider as a bright, attractive Danish woman in then-provincial Norway, she did not make friends easily, preferring her husband's professional male circle; she shocked neighbours and embarrassed her three daughters with her 'advanced' opinions on child-raising, and Sigrid Undset showed her mother's temper, well-stoked in her own comfortable childhood, frequently flaring up in *The Longest Years*. As Sigrid Undset observed, it was Charlotte's gift and misfortune to see things clearly in the spirit of eighteenth-century Enlightenment: 'To regard the world with the sanity of a rationalist and everything human with a benign suspicion — that was the ideal which for Anine [the name Sigrid Undset gave her mother in *The Longest Years*] was easier to possess than to practice' (quoted in Winsnes, *Sigrid Undset*, p. 15).

In one of life's common ironies, mother and daughter drew nearer to one another more closely as adults than they ever had been during Sigrid's youth. Sigrid Undset rejected the rationalism Charlotte tried to instil in her children, but Sigrid Undset's fiction reveals a growing respect for her mother's position that culminated in her last novel, *Madame Dorthea*, set in the eighteenth century. For her part, Charlotte Undset late in her life adopted the Roman Catholicism that Sigrid had embraced in 1924. Through her harsh early widowhood when Charlotte Undset was struggling to support and educate her daughters, she still managed to provide them with a cultured home life, and when Sigrid's first book, *Fru Marta Oulie*, was published in 1907, Charlotte proved how well she knew her daughter by inscribing a gift copy of Steen Steensen Blicher's *Birds of Passage* for her: 'May you as an author always look up to Blicher as your model, be as incorruptibly honest as he, fearlessly seeing life as it is and truthfully reporting what you see' (quoted in ibid., p. 2). A.H. Winsnes notes that Sigrid Undset sketched her mother as the widowed Mrs Wegener in her fourth novel, *Spring*, 1914: "'. . . she fostered the minds and thoughts of her children, from the poetry that filled her, [with] a transcendent richness and splendour, which her children sucked greedily in"' (quoted in ibid., p. 16).

Kalundborg: 1882–4

Sigrid Undset shaped 'In the Beginning', the opening section of *The Longest Years*, exquisitely, but some suspension of disbelief is necessary to accept a child's recollections prior to the age of two. Her American biographer Carl Bayerschmidt reasonably points out 'an element of "Dichtung und Wahrheit"' in *The Longest Years* and adds that since the Undsets frequently spent summer holidays at Kalundborg, Charlotte's maternal aunt, a talented storyteller, may have told the child tales of her earliest youth so often that Sigrid may have come to believe 'that they were part of her own conscious experience'.[8]

None the less, one of the earliest and most permanent experiences any child has is its name, so intimate a part of its identity and self-image that primitive societies connect knowledge of one's name with power over that individual. Sigrid Undset gave the child she had been the name 'Ingvild', a feminisation of her father's name, Ingvald, and to Ingvild/Sigrid '. . . all names that began with Ing were yellow. Inger was mustard-yellow, but Ingeborg was a pretty name which reminded one of a yellow rose shading to pink, and Ivar was like a ripe cornfield' (Undset, *The Longest Years*, pp. 6–7). Children quite commonly associate nouns with colours, but this child connected the prefix 'Ing', another name for the Norse fertility god Freyr, with the colours of plants in which she already was taking a unusual interest and the sun that makes them grow, as well as with the father Sigrid Undset loved so deeply. 'Ingvild was another yellow name. . . . On some people's lips it was a charming, downy light yellow shading to pale green, like a primrose. But . . . at school, she thought it recalled the dull yellow of wet clay' (ibid., p. 7). The mythic resonances of Ingvild/Sigrid's sensitivity to names may represent the child's unconscious responses to her surroundings or the mature author's means of evoking a reader's archetypal responses, or even both simultaneously; but certainly as a child Sigrid Undset already possessed remarkable perceptions of language and colour which became integral to her vivid literary style.

Not a memory but a piece of cherished family history provides another linguistic hint at a truth deeper than a child could realise, the eighteen-month-old Ingvild/Sigrid's mispronunciation of the Norwegian '*Glaedelig Jul*' ('Merry Christmas') as '*Graedelig* Jul'. Arthur Chater, translator of *The Longest Years*, indicates in a note on p. 7 that no such word as '*graedelig*' exists in Norwegian. He suggests 'tearful', from the Dano–Norwegian *Graad*, 'weeping'. Charlotte Undset's mother had died very young on a Christmas Eve, making it the saddest holiday of the year for the Gyths, and the child's uncanny mistake became a part of their family tradition.

The spring that she was a year old, Ingvild/Sigrid's father came home, a not-quite-thirty-year-old archaeologist bursting with enthusiasm for his work. Letters discovered many years later indicate that like many fathers, he imagined that his eldest child would carry on his work. He let her play with a little terracotta horse Schliemann had sent him from Troy, 'because it amused him [Ingvald Undset] to think that here was his little baby patting with her damp and podgy hands a toy which perhaps some Trojan child had caressed thousands of years ago' (ibid., p. 11). The little horse had its own symbolism that adults might see when a child would not; the Greeks fatally betrayed the trust of the horse-taming Trojans, a hint at griefs caused for Sigrid Undset by adults who, unknowingly or otherwise, violated a child's implacable concept of truth.

Just before her little sister was born, her father gave Ingvild a puppy, Bimbo, and together Bimbo and baby provided Ingvild/Sigrid's 'first great disappointment' (ibid., p. 17): the realisation that adults did not always tell the truth; that storks did not bring babies; and worse, although 'they had said that Bimbo was *her* dog'[italics in original], Bimbo, 'a part of her own restless, dawning ego', was given away. In Ingvild/Sigrid 'the first feeling of revolt was smouldering' (ibid., p. 18).

The House Near Vestre Aker Church, Oslo: 1884–6

In 1884 the Undset family moved to Christiania (renamed Oslo in 1925) so that Ingvald Undset could be near his work in the archaeological section of the University Museum. He sometimes awakened Ingvild/Sigrid to show her off to visiting colleagues — she had a particular distaste for an unkempt German scholar who smothered her with crumb-and-eggy kisses — and Ingvald often gave his daughter the run of the Museum, where the professor with whom he worked decked her in Viking grave-goods, big neck-rings of twisted gold and bracelets and rings that dwarfed her tiny fingers.

Ingvald and Sigrid also took long walks in the countryside outside Oslo, where he described flowers and plants so vividly she never forgot them. She made him explain the weather flags that flew atop St Hans' Hill nearby, which she childishly believed had 'something to do with God' (ibid., p. 53), a deity that she then thought was filled with capricious wrath: 'When she saw the triangle hoisted alone, the sunshine and the clear blue sky seemed like God's goodwill [sic]. . . . But the square was a sign that . . . He was in a bad temper and had turned away' (ibid., p. 57). When her father took her up St Hans' Hill a little later, she felt 'a certain sense of dread and awe of something overpowering' and 'she continued to think of St. Hans' Hill as a place which in some way or other was hallowed, and what hallowed it was something that was opposed to the security of home' (ibid., pp. 57–8). Sigrid Undset continued to experience this religious sense of God-in-nature throughout her life.

The trust Ingvild/Sigrid felt in the people closest to her had been shaken by another in the inexorable chain of contradictions of what she knew to be true, a process adults generally dismiss as 'growing up', having forgotten how real its pains always are. She had been delightedly visiting the beehives in the garden of the house where she lived until a horrified adult stopped her, a devastating blow to her sense of self: '. . . . Just as she became interested in something that filled her whole being with joy . . . the grown-ups would come and tell her that without knowing the least thing about it she had run the most frightful risk' (ibid., pp. 33–4).

10 Lyder Sagens Street, Oslo: 1886–91

Sigrid Undset called the four years she lived at 10 Lyder Sagens Street her 'real childhood' (ibid., p. 68). The house stood just at the edge of the countryside, and much later she recalled she felt there a mystic sense of Nature as a living entity: 'a huge body . . . arching itself in the light of dawn . . . in the noon heat it breathed and stared at us. . . . And in the evening . . . [it] heaved out strange sounds as it dreamed' (quoted in Winsnes, *Sigrid Undset*, p. 16).

While she lived at Lyder Sagens Street, Ingvild/Sigrid also gradually discovered the order that Nature imposed on her little universe, as well as important truths about human behaviour, through the myths that her father was teaching her to recognise, and the Undsets' German neighbours the Wilsters at first seemed to her like embodiments of natural forces. Ingvild spent hours with Herr Wilster while he tended his trees and rosebushes, and he reminded her of a thunder-god, familiar from pictures of Zeus and Jupiter in her father's Italian album. 'At times he [Herr Wilster] would rage . . . when his own swarm of children had produced chaos indoors and out and when he wanted to do some work . . . [but he gave away] rare and costly flowers when he was in a good humour' (Undset, *The Longest Years*, p. 88).

Frau Wilster, the imperturbable German-born French mother of fourteen children, could not have been more different from Charlotte Undset. Looking back, Sigrid Undset saw that Frau Wilster 'gave of herself as a prodigal, who never thinks of where the wealth comes from' (ibid., p. 87). The Nordic woman, Sigrid Undset observed, has a different nature; she '*sees* herself, her ego as it were her capital [her italics] . . . that self is never quite absent from her consciousness' (ibid., p. 86), even though she may choose to devote herself wholly to her husband and family.

Soon Ingvild/Sigrid's carefree world began to change, however; after Ingvald Undset had made an extensive research trip from Hamar to the remote Valdres area in 1888 with his old friend Henrik Mathiesen, Ingvald's health began to deteriorate. His earlier illness had left permanent disabilities, and he needed his wife's help more and more to assemble his books, the small popular study *The First Beginnings of the Oslo Valley*, published in 1890, and his memoirs, *From Akershus to the Acropolis*, which he worked on from 1888 to 1892, and which Norwegians still find highly readable. Not surprisingly under the circumstances, Charlotte's perfectionism and frustrations caused some tension in the family; she would pull out the little girl's clumsy stitchery and made work for herself with interminable handicrafts, but Ingvild/Sigrid showed an unusual understanding of her mother's real problem: if Charlotte 'so often spoke and acted unwisely, it was not infrequently due precisely to her being intelligent' (ibid., p. 89). It must have been far easier for a four-year-old, however, to enjoy the placid company of Frau Wilster, whose outline in the child's memory, like her jovial husband's, 'merged indistinctly in the picture of the clouds behind them and the trees and flowers with which they were surrounded' (ibid., p. 90).

The people she could not accept as 'powers of nature' caused disruptions in Ingvild/Sigrid's world, but at Lyder Sagens Street she learned to balance them against what she instinctively felt was right. She hated the deceit that she found in her aunt's fairy tales, like the story of the hedgehog who tricks the hare into forfeiting their race, because from the outset Sigrid Undset rebelled at injustice, however pragmatically successful its result might be. Far more to her taste were the immortal stories of Troy her parents were beginning to tell her; her first brush with the concept of tragedy was the legend of the curse on the house of Atreus with its fierce chain of murder and revenge, and it made so profound an impression on her that it continued to fascinate her for the rest of her life. Of all Greek tragedy, Aeschylus' *Agamemnon* most closely approaches the stark vengeance of the Old North which absorbed so much of Sigrid Undset's mature imagination.

For a child, it must have been difficult, if not impossible, to reconcile her parents' unorthodox theories of child-raising with her playmates' opinions of them, since children are notoriously hostile to anything or anyone set apart from their accustomed norms. One Christmas Ingvild received her heart's desire — a bobsled from her parents, skis from her Trøndelag grandpapa, and even the skates her father had had as a boy. All turned out to be hopelessly 'odd and wrong' in the other children's eyes, however, and no matter how strongly her father told her to ignore people who criticise things they know nothing about, Ingvild/Sigrid had to ski by herself to avoid her playmates' ridicule. 'She therefore became more or less reconciled to her fate' (ibid., p. 161).

Like all children of her time, Ingvild/Sigrid had been warned severely about mysterious matters she barely could grasp — why she should not take sweets from strangers: 'the beginnings of the sexual instruction from which no little girl is safe' (ibid., p. 176). Typically, all of it infuriated her. When she came across a man who exposed himself, she experienced 'a raging resentment against one who had imposed on her a loathsome and humiliating memory' (ibid., p. 176), and she recalled that like the rest of her young friends, she would have shied away from the well-meaning adult who might have tried to show them 'a purer and healthier view of the order of nature. . . . For they knew better' (ibid., p. 177).

As the mature writer who that child became, Sigrid Undset also knew the price of sexuality better than many of her contemporaries did. Even very young, she had preferred Ludwig Holberg's honest, earthy comedies which others called 'rude' to the trashy suggestive romances then in vogue, which she tolerated only when they were adventurous enough to be exciting. The seeds of the passionate sensuality that causes the tragic downfall of many of her heroines, from Jenny to Kristin Lavransdatter and even Madame Dorthea, appear in Sigrid Undset's own 'happy childhood', the title she gave that part of *The Longest Years* she spent at Lyder Sagens Street, where she already experienced that primal 'connection between the spasm of fear and the voluptuous feeling and the distraction which may come over one when one's body believes itself threatened with destruction, so that the blood runs wild and one does things of which one is afterwards terrified' (ibid., p. 179). Sigrid Undset's insight into female sexuality was controversial in her day. Neither in her own time nor the present have discussions of the subject often enjoyed her refreshing common sense. As a grown woman well into the Age of Freud, when she read 'that the many criminal and cruel manifestations of sexuality were merely the result of people having surrounded the instinct with a lot of deplorable tabu notions', she 'instinctively wondered how grown-up men can remain such five-year-old water carts' (ibid., p. 179).

Beyond the inevitable disappointments of growing up and the stresses of 'infant sexuality' in her 'happy childhood', Ingvild/ Sigrid's chief conflict lay in her developing sense of morality. Her home was periodically filled with young aunts and uncles discussing radical politics, 'the Right and the Left, and the High Court and Bjørnson and Sverdrup' (ibid., p. 209). Sverdrup resigned as Prime Minister in 1890 in the conflict over Swedish governance of Norway. Ingvild/Sigrid's Danish mother found the Norwegians took themselves 'so frightfully seriously. Where she came from, people fussed a great deal less about each other's affairs' (ibid., p. 208). On the other hand, Ingvald Undset could be a Roman in Rome easily enough, 'But he did compare Christiania with Trondhjem [sic], and not at all to the former's advantage' (ibid., p. 209).

Ingvild herself hated most of all 'being corrected in a friendly, decided tone . . . she did bear a grudge — a stubborn, invincible grudge — against those grown-ups who took it upon themselves to admonish her . . . in a rational and instructive spirit' (ibid., p. 111). The most important lesson she learned at Lyder Sagens Street was 'that it wasn't so easy to keep truth and untruth apart' (ibid., p. 210), and when her father punished her — very gently, one suspects — for telling lies about her sister, she had to contemplate moral problems for the first time in earnest. Later when Ingvald helped her with her lessons from *Legends and Tales of Antiquity*, she suddenly realised that not only 'the great figures who were to thrill her imagination must always do what was noble and right, unconditionally, even if it meant their ruin and death' (ibid., p. 191), but that the price truth demanded applied to her eight-year-old self as well.

Quite literally, a snake put an end to Ingvild's innocence in her Lyder Sagens Street garden. Not recognising it, she leaped over a live adder in the road one day. Everyone greeted her tale with horror, making her 'vaguely indignant': '. . . it was as though she had been betrayed, she didn't know by what, in that she had not guessed, the moment she saw the black ribbon, that *now* was the time to be afraid' (italics in original) (ibid., p. 224).

Such breaches of faith marked the child Ingvild and the woman she became. At Lyder Sagens Street and on summer holidays at Kalundborg, Trondheim, and Drøbak there were some shining golden moments when she followed Herr Wister about his flowerbeds, and when her father or mother ignited her imagination with the old stories that never die, and when a boy named Olav brought her apples and called her by her name. But the record Sigrid Undset made of small betrayals she suffered shows her growing distrust of the adult world, making 'Happy Childhood' a far less idyllic title than those words generally imply.

5 Keyser Street: 1891–2

As though to underscore the mounting gravity of her father's illness, Sigrid Undset called 5 Keyser Street, where the family moved in 1891, 'the House with the Dark Cellars', chilly and unpleasant-smelling, and Ingvald and Charlotte were so occupied with their own affairs that Sigrid had 'to play alone or with undesirable children, to make things with my hands or fancy stories out of my head' (*Twentieth Century Authors*, p. 1,432). More disappointments waited when she entered the third class of Ragna Nielsen's Liberal 'middle' school, the first coeducational school in Norway, which her parents had chosen 'only because they believed still less in the conservative girls' schools' (ibid., p. 1,432). School interfered with her freedom, and she hated it immediately: 'From the first day her attitude to the school and all that pertained to it was — or became — unfriendly.' (Undset, *The Longest Years*, p. 234).

However liberal Fru Nielsen's political persuasions were, her school stressed rote learning, elocution and the same fairy tales and sentimental novels Ingvild already detested. The work itself was far easier than her lessons at home had been, and she quickly grew bored when she saw that she knew more about a subject than her books could tell her. Worse yet, she soon began to realise that her teachers and her books, supposedly her new authorities, pretended to knowledge they did not and should not have. Her father had instilled in her the genuine scholarly method: '. . . even if we now think we know something with certainty . . . one fine day somebody or other may make discoveries which throw a new light on the whole question, and we shall be forced to go into it again from the beginning' (ibid., p. 237). Even if Ingvild/Sigrid had heard her father describe a view as 'entirely untenable', she was forced to repeat it at school as if it were true, and inevitably 'a teacher's having said a thing was enough to make her hesitate to accept it' (ibid., p. 237).

Charlotte had been sceptical about the Nielsen school — Sigrid Undset recalled in 1940 that her 'mother was always skeptical about everything' (*Twentieth Century Authors*, p. 1,432) — and she added to her daughter's discomfort by dressing her practically but unfashionably in boy's breeches under her skirts and knitted sweaters, and by letting her hair hang loose 'so that the air could get at the roots' (Undset, *The Longest Years*, p. 239). Such explosions as ensued when Ingvild told her mother that the writing teacher had suggested that she tie her hair up hardly made the child like school any better.

In self-defence, Ingvild/Sigrid became a 'regular bookworm' at home that winter, devouring Lapp fairy tales, Holberg's stories, and even the six formidable volumes of the Daae and Drolsum *History of the World* her father gave her two crowns to read. The task took her more than two years. She even borrowed adventure stories from her uncle and popular romances from the maid, which she read surreptitiously in her room at night. Nothing she ever read, however, made the impression on her that the Old

Icelandic *Njal's Saga* did when she came upon a translation of it the next summer at her grandfather's home in Trondheim, and she later called it the book that changed her life.

Njal's Saga, a thirteenth-century novel tracing forty years of tenth-century revenge, is widely considered to be the height of perfection in the ancient art of storytelling; it contains an immense variety of subplots and characterisations and an equally vast number of individual struggles in the difficult transition from a pagan to a Christian culture. For Ingvild/Sigrid, who frequently 'had to put the book down in order as it were to swallow what she had been reading' (ibid., p. 282), one character above all the rest was hypnotic: Skarphedin, the oldest son of the good Njal who dies in flames to keep faith with a friend. Skarphedin is no forgiving Christian; he is Odin's own pale warrior, touched by fate and able to defy it, chanting poetry as he draws flaming tragedy down around himself. Ingvild/Sigrid 'felt it had to be so — he was so impatient of everything in the world about him that he wanted to put an end to it all' (ibid., p. 282); she never forgot him. Several of her heroes, especially Erlend Nikulausson who captured Kristin Lavransdatter's heart to her grief and his own, and Olaf Audunsson, the handsome doomed master of Hestviken, owe much of their dangerous irresistible appeal to Skarphedin of the *Njála*.

Ingvild/Sigrid oddly pictured Skarphedin's face as rather like her pious grandfather's, 'sallow, with dark eyes and a dark beard', as he lay dying that summer at Trondheim. His rocklike piety frightened her a little: 'There was something terrible in the thought that a man could *love* God as grandfather did' (ibid., p. 267). In the face of such a love, lukewarm Christianity seemed as contemptible as the notion of a vindictive judgemental God. She felt that 'He was more dangerous and incomprehensible than that, and most incomprehensible was His love' (ibid., pp. 267–8). Ingvild/Sigrid was beginning to sense the necessity of all-consuming sacrifice that leads some believers to Christ; she saw that '[grandfather] had given himself to God without reserve' (ibid., p. 268), just as the Old Norse warriors had flung themselves gladly into Odin's arms.

She saw another side to religion in her Trondheim grandmother, whose faith made her unfailingly cheerful and good-humoured, unusual qualities among Norwegians. 'Whenever in [later] life Ingvild heard people blame Christianity for making men gloomy and cheerless and censorious, she thought . . . it was more probably . . . [because] very many Norwegians are melancholy at heart and by nature prone to distrust both their fellow-men and God himself' (ibid., pp. 289–90). Ingvild/Sigrid seems to have shared these dark qualities, since her general distrust of school included a distinct aversion to 'optimistic babble about a faith in the victory of goodness and a hope of a bright future'. While she instinctively reverenced the God she sensed in nature and in all good things, she had no desire for Him to take a personal concern in her. 'Without suspecting it, she wished for a God like the gods of the pagans' (ibid., p. 263). Sigrid Undset's journey toward Christian faith may have begun in 'the House with the Dark Cellars', but it was hardly Norway's conventional Lutheranism. Out of curiosity, she visited an Oslo church that winter alone, coming away shocked at the gulf between those who followed the letter of the law and her grandparents, whose vital faith sustained them. At ten years old, she already knew the difference.

Observatory Street: 1892–3

When the Undsets moved yet again, to Observatory Street near the Lyder Sagens house she had loved so dearly, Ingvild/Sigrid had to confront a shattering reality: her father's life was slipping away. Just before they had left Keyser Street, she had made up an outlandish Wild West tale to amuse him, and now she put what she called her 'devilish turn for languages' to use reading to him from his scholarly journals, from articles in the new *landsmål* then coming into wider use, and even from the Old Norse sagas, where sometimes 'she forgot all else in the chilling beauty of the verse'. Henrik Mathiesen, who had illustrated several of her father's articles and books, was visiting frequently since Ingvald had not yet given up his work, and when Mathiesen taught Ingvild/Sigrid to use artistic perspective, she was so delighted at being able to draw 'what she really *saw*, not what she knew to be there [italics in original] . . . [that] she forgot she ought to read to papa' (ibid., p. 305). He said nothing, but later she was tormented by guilt at neglecting him, and she more than atoned for it in portraying

Ingvald Undset as Kristin's saintly father Lavrans Björgulfsson.

The poverty the Undsets knew in Observatory Street weighed heavily on Ingvild/Sigrid; she resented the need which drove her mother to take money from their friends for a summer vacation, and she detested the money-grubbing hypocrisy of the people who lived around them, 'people who appeared to think the most important thing in life was to be taken for what one was not' (ibid., p. 308). Ingvild/Sigrid was ashamed when her mother had to ask for cheap things in the shops, or to leave without buying; and worse, the child was ashamed of being ashamed; 'she saw quite clearly that the most cheerless form of poverty is that which unprotestingly bows to the opinion that to be poor is a disgrace' (ibid., p. 310). Physical poverty led her to reject others' concepts of God and to see that her own concept of Him had no more validity than theirs; at this painful point in her life, Sigrid Undset confessed later, 'she believed nothing' (ibid., p. 314).

Ingvald Undset died in December 1893. For a while Charlotte Undset and her three daughters went daily to his grave, where '[the] grinning mound of yellow clay showed through more and more' (ibid., p. 327), a visible reminder of mortality that Sigrid even connected with the 'Ing' name she loved. Once they brought a laurel wreath sent by Ingvald's closest friend in Denmark; its ribbon bore some runes, 'and underneath in Danish: "Few better will come after"', a faithful Viking wife's inscription to her dead husband on an ancient Tryggevaelde gravestone. It brought Ingvild/Sigrid an enormous insight: 'among all the forgotten dead there had always been some whose loss their nearest and dearest thought irreparable and of whom they said: "Few better will come after". And then they went on living' (ibid., pp. 327–8).

Most of the Undsets' furniture went that January; the books followed. Charlotte Undset and her daughters moved again, to a crowded little apartment in Steen Street. Ragna Nielsen offered the girls free tuition through two years at her gymnasium, but at fifteen Ingvild/Sigrid resolved to leave school. Much later, she confessed that she had feared going to the University, because she would have had to become a teacher, 'and the very idea of a schoolroom was hateful to me' (*Twentieth Century Authors*, p. 1,432). She wanted to paint, but there was no money; 'Mother told me, since I had thrown away Fru Nielsen's offer I must learn something which would enable me to earn my own livelihood as soon as possible to help her provide for my younger sisters' (ibid., p. 1,432). In 1898, Sigrid Undset graduated from Oslo's Commercial College: 'Now that papa was dead there was no one on whom she cared to be dependent' (Undset, *The Longest Years*, p. 329).

Like Norway itself, a nation that had struggled through savage individualism in its Viking youth and groped after a new faith which it could reconcile with its melancholy nature, then suffering years of domination at others' hands, Sigrid Undset had to make her own way in the world; and now suddenly, paradoxically, at eighteen she was happy: 'It seemed to her that she already knew so much that was evil in the world and so much that was boundlessly good that it was all beyond her ... she could hardly bear such happiness' (ibid., pp. 331–2).

Notes

1. Sigrid Undset, *The Longest Years*, trans. Arthur G. Chater (New York: Knopf, 1935).
2. A.H. Wisnes, *Sigrid Undset: A Study in Christian Realism*, trans. P.G. Foote (New York: Sheed and Ward, 1953), p. 11. This study is cited in the text as Wisnes, *Sigrid Undset*.
3. Stanley J. Kunitz and Howard Haycroft (eds.), *Twentieth Century Authors* (New York: H.W. Wilson, 1942; 7th printing 1973), pp. 1,431. This work is cited hereafter in the text.
4. Carl Bayerschmidt, *Sigrid Undset* (New York: Twayne, 1970), p. 21.

3 Norwegian Women in Love: 1898–1911

> Man's love is of man's life a thing apart,
> 'Tis woman's whole existence.
>
> Lord Byron, *Don Juan*

Youth is traditionally a time to seek out one's calling, one's voice, one's self, and the ten years Sigrid Undset worked in an Oslo office made her a writer. Her decision not to pursue art had been reinforced by the well-known artist Theodor Kittelsen, whom she had met in the summer of 1894 at Drøbak; he believed the work a painter produces never equals the work that he had dreamed, and he discouraged her from 'a journey which leads to no goal'. The traveller bent on art, Kittelson told her, '. . . experiences nothing but humiliation, poverty, and intrigue [because] . . . Talent may be a gift, but it is also a curse'.[8] Kittelsen's words might have made Sigrid Undset think about her talented mother, using up hours in make-work handicrafts to keep herself from remembering what might have been. In any case, after Sigrid Undset received her secretarial certificate in 1899 she managed to find a clerical position with the German Electric Company in Oslo, where her conscientiousness and accurate memory made her a valued employee for ten years.

Sigrid Undset called this 'the beginning of my career as an author' and she claimed that she 'never looked upon this situation as anything but temporary',[2] but she had to work there until her two sisters became self-supporting. Convinced that she would eventually leave the office, she came to like it and her co-workers, and Oslo became her spiritual as well as a physical home: 'I had roots everywhere in this earth which I had trodden all the while I was growing up'.[3]

In Oslo, ancient and modern history enfolded Sigrid Undset. In the first decade of the new century, it was still called Christiania, a lovely city of 200,000 people living mainly on the west bank of the Aker River at the head of the Oslofjord, near the open water of the Skaggerak. To the south lay Drøbak, Oslo's winter port and the summer resort where the Undsets often took their holidays. Dark pine-covered hills, still popular for skiing, rise steeply behind the city, which looks out over islands in the fjord, and the Akershus fortress, until 1719 a royal palace originally established by Haakon V after he declared Oslo the capital of Norway in 1299, occupies the promontory between the city's two harbours. Old Oslo, founded in 1048 by Harold Sigurdsson, had burned in 1624, and the same year Christian IV of Denmark and Norway built his namesake city on its present site across the Aker. Facing the National Theatre, built in 1899 on Oslo's main street, the Karl-Johansgade, is the University of Oslo, established in 1811, and to the north is the Folk Museum of Norse Antiquities where Ingvald Undset had so briefly worked. The Museum houses the Oseberg and Gokstad Viking ships unearthed in 1867 and 1880, and at the time of writing Sigrid Undset's niece Charlotte Blindheim serves as a curator there. In 1910, Sigrid Undset described Oslo as 'the most beautiful town in the world, its people the most delightful, their speech, in its every nuance from Homansby to Ekeberg, the most joyous means of expression for human thought' (quoted in Bayerschmidt, *Sigrid Undset*, p. 27).

Although she had to work as a secretary, literature offered Sigrid Undset the noble means of educating herself. First, typically, she looked to the literature of her own country, and at the turn of the century, Norway was conquering literary Europe. Ibsen and Bjørnson, Jonas Lie, Gunnar Heiberg and Amalie Skram were all opening — sometimes breaking — windows long closed in literature, letting brisk Northern air strip artifice and hypocrisy from the most profound social and psychological issues that affect men and women. Young Sigrid Undset was especially taken with Ibsen's *The Wild Duck*, 1884, an enigmatic play whose central issue is the value of truth in human life. The central figure of *The Wild Duck* is Gregers Werle, whose blind idealistic insistence on truth as he alone sees it leads to the tragic death of the adolescent girl Hedwig. The play also contains a vivid portrait of a superficially charming but inherently weak man, Hjalmar Ekdal, whose shallowness evokes contempt. In *The Wild Duck* Ibsen seems to conclude that since man is too weak to endure the truth, he must live a lie to sustain his existence, a runic comment on the human condition that must have intrigued Sigrid Undset deeply.

34

She had also discovered the study *William Shakespeare*, written by the Danish realistic critic Georg Brandes in 1895–6, and with the same grit she had shown by working through the multivolume *History of the World*, she set about reading 'everything that had been written in English' (quoted in Winsnes, *Sigrid Undset*, p. 33), which she nearly accomplished, as far as English classics are concerned. From Shakespeare she branched out into the heady air of Elizabethan literature, and then she devoured English novels, savouring Fielding's lusty handsomely crafted novels and Dickens' Victorian panoramas. English Romantic poetry also captivated Sigrid Undset as a young woman, and according to Charlotte Blindheim, the poems of Keats, Shelley and Emily Brontë were still 'very dear to her heart' when Undset became older:

> Her voice often grew tremulous when she read lines like those of Emily Brontë [from 'The Prisoner']:
>> Still, let my tyrants know, I am not doomed to wear
>> Year after year in gloom, and desolate despair,
>> A messenger of hope comes every night to me
>> And offers for short life eternal liberty.
>> Then dawns the Invisible, the Unseen its truth reveals;
>> My outward sense is gone, my inward essence feels:
>> Its wings are almost free, its home, its harbor found,
>> Measuring the gulf, its stoops and dares the final bound.[4]

As a girl with a brilliant mind and only her own two hands to provide her intellectual as well as material nourishment, Sigrid Undset must often have felt trapped in 'year after year of gloom' at her office job. She commented in 1940: 'Above all things I had always desired liberty to do what I wanted. But ever since my seventeenth year I have always had to consider somebody else's interests, whatever I have been doing' (*Twentieth Century Authors*, p. 1433). Her means of escape began in 1908, when she fictionalised her predicament in a short story, 'The Happy Age': '"We carry on and find a job which allows us to live — we can't live *for* it"' (italics in original) (quoted in Winsnes, *Sigrid Undset*, p. 37). Her long nights of reading helped her achieve an 'eternal liberty', for she soon became passionately devoted to the Middle Ages, when English and Scandinavian literature were bound closely together by common linguistic ancestry, Germanic customs and their religious heritage. She savoured Chaucer's works, the medieval ballads of England and Norway, and the German *minnesingers'* songs, and over and over she read the Old Norse myths and sagas. At eighteen Sigrid Undset flabbergasted an Oslo librarian by asking for Ungar's *Stories and Legends of Holy Men and Women*, which had not been checked out since its publication in 1877 (ibid., p. 34).

Caught up in the spell of the past, Sigrid Undset was not only reading but writing as well, working at her job and her literary pursuits together about eighteen hours a day. In a letter to Dea Forsberg, her Swedish correspondent at the time, she mentioned that she was writing a novel of thirteenth-century Norway, an early version, as it turned out, of *The Master of Hestviken*. 'Trembling with apprehension', she took the manuscript to the Gyldendal publishing firm, whose director, Peter Nansen, sympathetically suggested: '"Don't try your hand at any more historical novels. It's not your line. But you might, you know, try to write something modern. One can never tell!"' (ibid., p. 34). Had Nansen known Sigrid Undset as the child who balked at fairy-tale deceit and the hypocrisy of a school that refused to search out the truth, and the eleven-year-old who was smitten by the *Njála*, he might have spoken differently. In any case, Sigrid Undset went home, her thoughts whirling, and began to write something altogether new: '"I have been unfaithful to my husband"'. That, she felt, 'should be modern enough' (ibid., pp. 34–5). *Fru Marta Oulie*, the novel she thus began, was at first rejected by the Aschehoug Publishing Company, but Sigrid's youngest sister Signe suggested she send it to the prominent Oslo dramatist Gunnar Heiberg, probably the most moralistic of the late-nineteenth-century Norwegian writers and an Oslo man with the special Oslo tone: 'a tendency to conceal a warm heart behind a reserved exterior'.[5] In 1897 Heiberg had forcefully expressed his national idealism in *The People's Council*, a play in which he criticised the Storthing's overcaution in its dealing with Sweden, and he used a female character to embody the moral integrity he felt his country needed. When Sigrid Undset sent her manuscript to him, Heiberg had recently completed his most powerful play, *The Tragedy of Love*, a dramatisation of the conflict between woman's love and man's work, and he recognised a kindred spirit in Sigrid Undset. Heiberg's generous recommendation persuaded Aschehoug to publish *Fru Marta Oulie* in the autumn of 1907, launching Sigrid Undset's literary career.

Fru Marta Oulie ('Mrs Marta Oulie')[6]

The first sentence of this novel brutally announces Sigrid Und-set's theme of marital infidelity, a variety of oath-breaking with reverberations in the Norwegian cultural consciousness, both ancient and modern. The Old Germanic bride was free to accept or reject her suitor, but once she received her husband's ring, an emblem of his honour set on his sword by his chieftain for prowess in battle, they were bound together by the oaths their tribes held most sacred. Betraying a sworn oath echoes down the ages as the worst infringement of moral law the Northern hemisphere knew, a lesson Ingvild/Sigrid had learned early in her life: keeping or betraying one's word showed the measure of a human being.

In the nineteenth century, however, literature was beginning to look into woman's role in marriage, questioning whether keeping an oath to one's husband must mean betraying one's self. Ibsen, who had died the year before *Fru Marta Oulie* appeared, had already dealt conventional attitudes two devastating blows, the slam of the Helmer front door on Nora's escape from *A Doll's House* in 1879 and ten years later the pistol shot with which Hedda Gabler, like an Old Norse hero, chose her own death over a life of subjugation to an inadequate husband, the vicious blackmailer Judge Brock, and an insufferably hypocritical society. By the 1900s, Gunnar Heiberg had seen a new way 'to champion the right of the individual as over against an obtuse and levelling democratic society ... he found an imperious, passionate love to be an end in itself'.[7] Since Sigrid Undset reacted against this view with her treatment of marital infidelity, Heiberg's championing of her work seems all the more remarkable.

Sigrid Undset, like many young writers, chose a diary form filled with flashbacks to illustrate the consequences of Marta Oulie's absorption in 'Love — there was nothing else in life worth living for!' (quoted in Winsnes, *Sigrid Undset*, p. 38). Marta's youthful feminism soon melts when she meets handsome Otto Oulie: 'God knows how glad I was to throw away the books and

37

run out into the bright world' (quoted in Bayerschmidt, *Sigrid Undset*, p. 55). However, when Otto proves faithful but dull, romantic love soon dwindles, and faced with the realities of marriage and three children, Marta flies into a purely physical affair with Otto's closest friend, Henrik. When Otto dies in a tuberculosis sanatorium without suspecting that she has betrayed him, Marta is consumed with self-loathing and rejects Henrik's offer of marriage. Finally, Sigrid Undset allows Marta the bitter insight that her own self-worship has cut her off from everyone — friend, husband, children and lover.

In his *Tragedy of Love*, Heiberg had pronounced the 'modern' liberal and strictly individualistic view of love; his heroine Karen asks: '"What does love have to do with houses, homes, and all that?"' (quoted in Gustafson, 'Christian Ethics', p. 301). The answer that Sigrid Undset forced Marta Oulie to see was, simply, 'Everything'. At this early point, Sigrid Undset was speaking from her entirely humanistic conviction that '[no] man is an island'; each individual, perhaps women even more than men, must seek fulfilment in others' happiness, most of all through their families. Although just before his death Otto found peace in traditional Christian belief, Marta could no more accept its answers than the 25-year-old Sigrid Undset could. Marta lamented that from the inside: '"Christianity is consistent enough . . . as though one were standing in a lofty cathedral with stained glass windows. If it were not . . . that the whole real world and the daylight are outside!"' (quoted in Bayerschmidt, *Sigrid Undset*, p. 57). Sigrid Undset explored the same question in her 1908 one-act play, 'In the Grey Light of Dawn', (not translated) from the point of view of a husband who leaves his home for a new marriage that also fails. The theme of marital infidelity never left Sigrid Undset's work, although many years were to pass before she viewed it in the steady glow of Christian faith.

Den lykkelige alder ('The Happy Age')

Like many of Sigrid Undset's titles, the name of her first collection of short fiction is ironic. Published in 1910, it contains two sketches, 'A Half-Dozen Handkerchiefs' and 'A Dream', and two short stories, 'A Stranger' and 'The Happy Age', none of which has been translated into English. Together, Carl Bayerschmidt remarks, they reveal Sigrid Undset's own 'heartaches and disappointments' during her adolescence (ibid., p. 58), which mothers and aunts call 'the happy age', having forgotten the pain those years usually involve.

The two sketches allowed Sigrid Undset to treat incidents from her own childhood with the unflinching honesty that became one of her hallmarks. In the bittersweet 'A Dream', she attempts to analyse dreams she had at ten and at sixteen, and in 'A Half-Dozen Handkerchiefs' she deals with the deceit that society often forces on an individual, in this case Bildit, a fictional little girl whose parents cannot afford the things they would like to give her. Bildit never complains, but she often makes up stories to excuse her situation to her classmates.

A.H. Winsnes calls this collection 'the most sensitive piece of writing about girlhood that has ever appeared in Norwegian . . . [and] nearest to reality' (Winsnes, *Sigrid Undset*, p. 43). Charlotte Hedels, heroine of the title story, voices the longing that was driving Sigrid Undset: '"I wanted to write about . . . all these half-lovely districts we respectable drudges live in . . . all the worn-out little words which we all let fall so carelessly . . . about you or myself or about any of us office-worms"' (quoted in ibid., p. 37).

The 'respectable drudges' with whom Sigrid Undset lived and worked represented a new social phenomenon in the early twentieth century, decent young women harnessed to dismal office jobs, going home to drab boarding houses, and dreaming of finding a love that could count the world well lost. Time after time, Sigrid Undset saw that when such hopes accompany high principles, ideals must painfully compromise with reality. She did allow one happy ending in this collection; Edele in 'A Stranger' yields to Alf because she pities his weakness. She is badly scarred by their inevitable break, but finds a better object for her love in Per, an old friend, who offers her the gift of genuine concern for others that allows her to accept his love at last.

In Charlotte of the story 'The Happy Age', however, Sigrid Undset poured out her own despondency: '"We all want the same thing . . . to live for one moment with our whole being turned inward . . . into our own burning hearts"' (quoted in Bayerschmidt, *Sigrid Undset*, p. 61); but self-absorption fails to satisfy Charlotte's yearning to worship something greater than a mortal man. Charlotte takes refuge in suicide, while her friend Uni, a fledgling actress whose story Sigrid Undset continued in 'Mrs Hjelde', 1917, achieves a little success in her career, despite her fiancé's old-fashioned opposition.

Unlike *Ungdom* ('Youth'), a collection of verse Sigrid Undset also published in 1910, which proved merely, Alrik Gustafson claims, 'that she had no lyric abilities at all' ('Christian Ethics', p. 305), *Fru Marta Oulie* and *Den lykkelige alder* ('The Happy Age') earned Sigrid Undset a respectable literary reputation in Norway for careful craftsmanship and what Gustafson describes as 'a curious combination of youthful disillusion and idealism that was usually rather intriguing in its forthright, sombre manner' (ibid.).

Gunnar's Daughter

Sigrid Undset's next novel, *Gunnar's Daughter*, was less of a public and artistic success than *Fru Marta Oulie*. In 1910 she said in an interview that she was not yet completely comfortable with the thirteenth-century milieu she had used for her rejected early draft of *The Master of Hestviken* (Winsnes, *Sigrid Undset*, p. 40), but she felt on surer medieval ground after she wrote *Gunnar's Daughter*, set at the close of the tenth century, when Christianity had barely scratched the surface of the pagan cultures of Iceland and Norway. Like the *Njála* which had impressed her so deeply as a child, *Gunnar's Daughter* is a tale of revenge smouldering over many years in a splendidly barbaric setting, but whereas the saga depicts its actions objectively, allowing the reader the freedom to form his or her own conclusions, the tendency toward psychological analysis based on meticulous detail already evident in her work prevents Sigrid Undset from achieving a similar impact in this novel. Bayerschmidt accurately observes that *Gunnar's Daughter* is 'a tale written from the woman's point of view, and many of its passages, charged with emotion, are conceived in a style completely foreign to the saga' (*Sigrid Undset*, p. 67).

In the essay she later wrote about the *Njála*, 'A Book That Was a Turning Point in My Life', Sigrid Undset noted that in the world of the Icelandic saga, men whose society demanded personal vengeance rather than social responsibility for punishing crimes were often forced into the bitterest of choices between their own moral principles and their family obligations: 'The family unit, far from being a source of strength, actually set restrictions upon an individual's freedom of action and consequently placed him in a dilemma from which he was unable to extricate himself' (ibid., p. 63).

In *Gunnar's Daughter*, Sigrid Undset has Vigdis, the pagan daughter of Gunnar, a Norwegian chieftain, choose between revenge and love. Ljot, an Icelander, lodges with Gunnar during a trading trip to Norway. After three weeks he asks Vigdis to marry him, but while she hesitates Ljot and Gunnar fall out over a horse-fight. Ljot takes Vigdis by force, leaving her pregnant, and before he sails for Iceland, Vigdis curses him brutally: '"May you have the worst of deaths — and live long and miserably — you and all you hold dear. And may you see your children die a most wretched death before your eyes"' (quoted in ibid., p. 64).

In Iceland, Ljot marries Leikny, but he still loves Vigdis, whose savage words come to pass. All his children with Leikny perish: one as a little child, another deformed baby that soon dies, though Ljot, nominally a Christian, refuses to follow custom and expose it; two others drown as their father watches helplessly, and Leikny herself dies of grief in Ljot's arms. Meanwhile, Vigdis delivers her son secretly and abandons him in the forest, but after the child is saved by one of her thralls, Vigdis takes the boy back, raising him to be the instrument of her vengeance: '"Not lightly would he escape from the dog I reared with hate and blows, until he had his teeth in Viga-Ljot's throat"' (quoted in ibid., p. 64). Gunnar perishes attempting to avenge Vigdis' honour, and after killing her father's murderer, Vigdis presents her case to King Olav Tryggvasson, who protects her on condition that she and her son Ulvar ('wolf') be baptised.

When Ulvar makes a Viking expedition to Scotland, Ljot, not knowing that Ulvar is his son, saves Ulvar's life. They return to Norway as fast friends, where Vigdis reveals Ljot's identity and incites a duel between father and son. After Ljot nobly brings on his own death, Ulvar lays his father's grey head in his mother's lap and rides away. Vigdis Gunnarsdatter remained to live 'long and miserably', knowing that '". . . it was the worst of all, that I would rather have loved him than any man"'.[8]

Although in its tenth-century Old Norse trappings and the overwhelming physical force of Vigdis' revenge *Gunnar's Daughter* differs strikingly from her earlier published fiction, Sigrid Undset was still dealing with the same profound conflict of the female heart: duty to self was pitted against duty to others, and when Vigdis allows selfish motives to overcome her attachment to her lover and their son she loses them both. Religion offers no help to either protagonist in this icy tragedy; both Vigdis and Ljot have been baptised Christians out of less-than-pious motives, he because an old hermit demanded it as his price for healing Ljot's gangrenous wound and she because she needed Olaf Tryggvasson's help. Ljot proves the more generous soul in the context of his warrior's code, first by provoking the son he loved into their fatal duel so that Ulvar might satisfy Vigdis' demands, and then by falling on his own sword to save Ulvar from the guilt of parricide. Vigdis, once a pagan priestess, fatally believes neither in Thor of the oath-keepers nor in the forgiving Christ but in her own strength. This is the same mistake her father Gunnar had made before her and one that assures Vigdis' downfall just as certainly as Marta's and Charlotte's tragedies in Sigrid Undset's earlier fictional worlds, where she also demonstrated that personal revenge destroys the soul. Sigrid Undset left off writing about the Middle Ages for a decade after *Gunnar's Daughter*, but she must have known that she would later return to it; in 1910 she commented: 'When one peels off the layer of ideas and conceptions that belong essentially to one's own time, one steps straight into the Middle Ages' (quoted in Winsnes, *Sigrid Undset*, p. 42).

Sigrid Undset was twenty-seven when her younger sisters became self-supporting and she could give up her job at the German Electric Company to devote herself to full-time writing. She was corresponding with Nini Roll Anker,[9] a prominent Norwegian writer who, though born and married into Norway's upper class, was none the less deeply concerned with the conditions of working women. Mrs Anker's keen social conscience had motivated her novel *The Weaker Sex*, 1915, an attack on women's education as crippling women's sexual potential. Before they met when Sigrid Undset returned from her European trip in 1910, the two women had been exchanging letters for some time, sharing views on feminism and the suffragette movement which was winning Norwegian women the right to vote; most importantly, they concurred in rejecting the feminists' deprecation of motherhood. In her posthumous untranslated memoir, *Min venn Sigrid Undset* ('My Friend Sigrid Undset'), 1946, Mrs Anker described Sigrid Undset as she appeared in her late twenties: 'Everything about her stirred the imagination: the large eyes . . . which seemed as much turned inwards as outwards . . . the beautiful slender hands . . . the lazy voice . . . the strength and power of endurance which stood her in good stead later in life' (quoted in Winsnes, *Sigrid Undset*, p. 52).

In 1909, Sigrid Undset had obtained a travel grant from the Norwegian government and followed Ibsen's steps to Italy, travelling outside Scandinavia for the first time in her life. She intended to spend two months in Berlin, where she visited the headquarters of the company she had worked for in Oslo, but she had already developed a distate for Prussian arrogance. She wrote that the Germans: '"lived in an atmosphere of self-importance . . . convinced that whatever they do is the only right and proper thing to be done"' (quoted in ibid., p. 49).

From Berlin, she took the 'Romantic Road' south through Dinkelsbühl and Rothenburg ob der Tauber, ancient walled towns where the medieval atmosphere was far more to her taste than the vaunted *Berliner Luft*, and came to Rome, where she settled in a little flat in the Via Fratina among practising and hopeful Scandinavian artists and writers; one was Helene Fagstad from Lillehammer, whom Sigrid Undset entertained in Roman tavernas with tales of the Middle Ages. During that winter she also wrote travel sketches for the Oslo *Aftenposten*, and in one of them, 'Children of Ara Coeli' she recorded a sharp insight into the relationship between parents and their offspring that a children's Epiphany programme had produced: '"I don't believe that Italian parents ever discuss how they are to win the trust of their children. For then the children in Ara Coeli would scarcely have come forward and acted their parts with such wonderful confidence"' (quoted in ibid., p. 53).

She made an even more intimate acquaintance in Rome that winter, too; at Christmas of 1909 she met the Norwegian artist Anders Castus Svarstad, thirteen years her senior and already married to Ragna Moe, who had attended Ragna Nielson's school when Sigrid Undset was there. It would be two and a half years before Svarstad was free and they could be 'together for all time',[10] but meanwhile in that Roman spring Sigrid Undset sat for Svarstad, and her 27-year-old heart opened to its first burning love.

Letters Sigrid Undset sent from Paris in the summer of 1910 reveal her deepening preoccupation with women's rights and marriage. Although she had already begun to treat the problem in her fiction, her comments now seem less theoretical and more personal, even more passionately her own. Noting that progressive women's groups were demanding that customary injunctions like St Paul's 'Wives, be submissive to your husbands' be dropped from Norwegian marriage services, she mused about the risk women took by approaching the altar not wishing to hear them. 'For these selfsame words carry nature's own legal prescription for marriage: that a woman shall marry the man whom she can call her lord — and no one else' (quoted in Winsnes, *Sigrid Undset*, p. 56).

The man Sigrid Undset chose to call her lord remains a shadowy figure today. Until their marriage in early 1912, Sigrid Undset tried to keep her relationship with Svarstad a secret, although a few people in Oslo knew of it (Krane, *Sigrid Undset*, p. 39); Nini Roll Anker observed the strain her friend was under at the time, but once Sigrid Undset made her decision she did not budge from it. A.H. Winsnes, writing just before her death and certainly with regard for her feelings, describes Svarstad as 'a brusque headstrong man with bad nerves', a keen intelligence and the full courage of his convictions. When Sigrid Undset met him, Svarstad already had a formidable reputation as 'a painter with an extremely individual colour-sense and with the deepest respect for technical ability' (ibid., p. 58), and of his well-known pictures of east Oslo's industrial section like 'Factory Girl', 1902, and 'Myren's Workshop in Oslo, 1903', Winsnes remarks that 'evanescent qualities of loveliness have been immortalised, qualities not unlike those which Sigrid Undset has captured in her descriptions of poor grey surroundings in the city of her childhood and youth' (ibid., p. 58). Making biographical assumptions solely from works of art is notoriously an area where critics should fear to tread, but the novel Sigrid Undset produced in the summer of 1911 clearly reflects matters that must have been close to her heart at that time. The novel was *Jenny*, and that autumn it became the most talked-about book in Norway.

Jenny

Harald Beyer calls *Jenny* 'the great realistic novel of its period, a profound psychological study, written with painful intensity' (Beyer, 'Sigrid Undset', p. 306). In *Jenny*, Sigrid Undset explores nearly every possible aspect of women's love, from the frankly erotic and even the perverse to the soaring moral ideals that at last destroy Jenny Winge 'of the fair face and kind voice'.[11] Even today *Jenny* is a shocking novel, not so much for its revelations about female sexuality, common enough in post-sexual revolution literature, but for its startling range of perception and its conclusion that faith in oneself, however ennobling, is not enough for personal salvation.

Her protagonist, Jenny, is a tall attractive Norwegian artist (physically resembling Sigrid Undset) living in Rome. Her erratic friend Francesca, modelled to some degree on Helene Fagstad, is in the grip of a torrid love affair with a temperamental divorced pianist from Berlin, who brutalises her, takes up with other women, casts her off, and yet continues to exert an hypnotic power over her. Jenny, by contrast, sets for herself the highest moral standards. A newcomer, the callow archaeologist Helge Gram, dazedly wandering through his first visit to Rome, enters the little group Jenny and 'Cesca share with Lennart Ahlin, a sculptor, and Gunnar Heggen, an artist. Out of pity and an unconscious maternal urge, Jenny yields — just a kiss — to Helge, enough to drift them into a hazy engagement in the soft Roman spring, a relationship that inevitably withers in the stagnant air of Helge's home in Oslo, rank with his parents' bitter disillusion with one another and their marriage. At last Jenny realises that she has deceived Helge and worse, herself, and she breaks off their relationship; but Gert Gram, Helge's father, an unfulfilled artist himself, then offers her a man's love. Jenny 'did not want a lover, because she was expecting a master' (*Jenny*, p. 192), but she is 'sick with longing in her inmost heart behind the shield of opinions and thoughts which she had made for herself' (ibid, p. 191). She gives Gert her body, because she 'found it so severe and hard to live the life I considered the most healthy — so lonely, you see' (ibid., p. 264), but even after she realises she is pregnant, she cannot offer him her soul.

The climax of *Jenny* is a graphic description of the heroine's late pregnancy and the birth of her feeble little son, who dies a few weeks later. The rest of Jenny's story is a sad downward spiral into oblivion; sick at heart, the young woman returns to Rome but can no longer paint, and when Gunnar Heggen offers her the genuine love that might save her, Jenny shrinks from him. Helge visits her, unaware of her affair with his father, and when he forces himself on her, a pang of motherhood betrays her: '. . . she imagined she felt the dead little one caressing her, and it gave her a sensation of joy, so that her body relaxed for a second in his arms' (ibid., p. 289). Afterwards, '[she] saw her own body . . . white, bare, beautiful — a thing that she had flung away. . . . It was not hers any more' (ibid., p. 291). Alone and without hope in one of those paradoxes of life that art can only imitate, Jenny perishes in spite and because of her high ideals, while Francesca survives her obsession with a false master and finds fulfilment in a conventional marriage, giving up her attempt at art in order to bear Lennart Ahlin's child.

Alone in the Protestant Cemetery in Rome where Keats' body, Shelley's heart and now Jenny's corpse lie buried, Gunnar Heggen is left with sorrow that 'would forever be the inmost essence of his soul' (ibid., p. 296), a lesson Jenny and Sigrid Undset had borne in on him forever: 'No woman has given life to the child she dreamed of when she bore it — no artist has created the work he saw before him in the moment of his inspiration. . . . And no love is what lovers dreamed when they kissed for the first time' (ibid., p. 304). By setting Kittelsen's advice about art in the context of a woman in love, Sigrid Undset was beginning to shape the major message of her creative life.

The uproar over *Jenny* rocked Norway's literary scene. The novel enraged both the traditionalists, bound to take umbrage at its acceptance of women's sexual needs and its near-clinical descriptions of pregnancy and childbirth, and the feminists, who bridled at Sigrid Undset's insistence that woman cannot live by work or even by art alone. Even more unsettling to Norwegian feminists was Sigrid Undset's characterisation of Jenny as far more dependent on her sexuality than a man would be, which seemed to contradict the theory of equality between the sexes for which they were struggling. When the Oslo Club for Women's Suffrage met to discuss *Jenny* on 19 February 1912, Nini Roll Anker reported that the membership was 'seething with indignation' (quoted in Winsnes, *Sigrid Undset*, p. 57). Sigrid Undset herself was there, but she imperturbably took no part in the discussion. She later thought the meeting had been 'the essence of comedy . . . I sat and waited for them to start beating one another about the head with their handbags, but unfortunately it never got so far' (quoted in ibid., p. 57).

Later that spring, Sigrid Undset left Norway again. She married Svarstad in the office of the Norwegian consul in Antwerp, and the couple made their first home in Hammersmith, west London, where Svarstad painted and Sigrid Undset began her next collection of stories, prophetically titled *Fattige skjebner* ('Poor Fortunes').

Notes

1. Quoted in Carl Bayerschmidt, *Sigrid Undset* (New York: Twayne, 1970), p. 26.
2. Stanley J. Kunitz and Howard Haycroft (eds.), *Twentieth Century Authors* (New York: H.W. Wilson, 1942; 7th printing, 1973), p. 1433.
3. Quoted in A.H. Winsnes, *Sigrid Undset: A Study in Christian Realism*, trans. P.G. Foote (New York: Sheed and Ward, 1953), p. 31.
4. Quoted in Charlotte Blindheim, *Moster Sigrid. Et familie portrett av Sigrid Undset* (Oslo: Aschehoug, 1982); this passage is translated in an excerpt published in *The Scandinavian Review*, vol. 70, no. 2 (June, 1982), p. 53, which is cited hereafter.
5. Harald Beyer, 'Sigrid Undset', in Einar Haugen (ed.), *A History of Norwegian Literature*, trans. Einar Haugen, (New York: New York University Press, 1956), p. 254.
6. The Norwegian titles are used for works that have not been translated into English. Passages are cited in English translation from other sources.
7. Alrik Gustafson, 'Christian Ethics in a Pagan World', in *Six Scandinavian Novelists* (Minneapolis, Minn.: University of Minnesota Press), pp. 300–1.
8. Sigrid Undset, *Gunnar's Daughter*, trans. Arthur G. Chater (New York: Knopf, 1933), p. 272.
9. Sigrid Undset's correspondence with Nini Roll Anker is as yet unavailable in English in its entirety, but excerpts translated by Carl Bayerschmidt and A.H. Winsnes are cited here.

10. Borghild Krane, *Sigrid Undset. Liv og meninger* ('Sigrid Undset: [Her] Life and Opinions'; untranslated) (Oslo: Gyldendal, 1970), p. 29; my translation. This work is cited hereafter.
11. Sigrid Undset, *Jenny*, trans. W. Emmé (New York: Knopf, 1921), p. 19.

4 Poor Humanity: 1911–1919

> ... theirs is the kingdom of heaven.
> Matthew 5:10

Whatever dreams Sigrid Undset might have had about marriage in the spring of 1912, reality proved different. She had already supported herself and others for thirteen years; now aged thirty, she felt she knew her own mind: 'Above all things I had always desired liberty to do what I wanted' and she described her departure from office work as 'gaining my freedom'.[1] Ironically, the fiction and the essays she produced between 1912 and 1919 reveal that she was only exchanging one set of responsibilities for another, far more serious obligation.

Sigrid Undset and Svarstad spent most of 1912 in England, and according to her biographers this was probably the most carefree time in her life. Her likes and dislikes were clear; she loved the beautiful English countryside and Webster's intense Jacobean drama captured her imagination, as she commented to Nini Roll Anker: '. . . these burning, flaming outbursts, centuries old though they are, can enthrall us so absolutely and so miraculously'.[2] Sigrid Undset and Svarstad often visited art galleries, and she dismissed most of the Post-Impressionists as 'frightening humbug', preferring to watch the gallery-goers who wandered around 'trying to look gifted'.[3]

While Svarstad was painting, Sigrid Undset became absorbed with the relations between the sexes, possibly because married life did not seem to be fulfilling her expectations. She told Mrs Anker: 'I shall never feel like a properly married woman', calling herself one of those 'lonely unmarried women who have never known what happiness is, unless they perchance find it in some irregular or secret love'.[4]

Fattige skjebner ('Poor Fortunes')

Sigrid Undset completed *Fattige skjebner*, a collection of short stories, in London. She was beginning to distance herself from her characters to a greater degree than she had in her earlier fiction, but she maintained her profound sympathy for humble people struggling to maintain their dignity against society's formidable odds, something she herself had experienced first hand during her years in Oslo.[5]

'Selma Brøter' (1912) belonged to that group of 'lonely unmarried women' Sigrid Undset could not believe she had left. Life for Selma, a thirtyish spinster, had been a succession of dingy boarding houses and a stifling office job brightened only when her co-workers Stener Gundersen, a young architect, and Beate Nordahl, a secretary, fall in love and use the unsuspecting Selma as a decoy for their meetings. Beate leaves her job to marry Stener and their baby arrives a bit too soon, but they are blissfully happy despite the office gossip in which only Selma refuses to join. When Selma's sister Alvilde is left widowed and pregnant, Selma sacrifices herself as she always has to her family's needs, caring for Alvilde's child so that her sister can find a new life for herself. Selma contents herself with a tangle of sad fabrications and might-have-beens, pathetic spinsterish imaginings that, however empty, are her only source of self-respect.

In this story, Sigrid Undset for the first time underscored a view of the female predicament that she maintained throughout the rest of her work: '"We do know how terrible life can be. And yet it's infinite happiness to have . . . children"', Beate claims, blessed, as the name Sigrid Undset gave her implies, with her child and its father's love. Selma has to make do with the hand-me-down happiness she finds in caring for her sister's child, but Sigrid Undset tempered the pathos with saving irony. '"Hell, if I was quite sure she'd refuse me I'd propose to her", said old Møller, whose pity Selma mistook for interest. '"Nobody else will, and it's damned hard luck on a woman to be an old maid without even having had the chance to turn somebody down"' (*Four Stories*, p. 56). Even though Møller never brings himself to take the risk, he shows the same rough male physical insight Stener voices later: '"It's a shame . . all she'll ever know of lovemaking will be some fellow or other talking to her in the street"' (ibid., p. 58). Beate is less compassionate, telling Stener that being needed makes Selma '"happier than she's ever been in her whole life"' (ibid., p. 59). Sigrid Undset closes the story on a note new in her fiction, Stener's tentative admission of Divine Purpose: '"Perhaps that's what's meant by 'all things work together for good to them that love God'"' (ibid., p. 59).

No compensation lightens the wretchedness of the title character in 'Miss Smith-Tellefsen' (1912), a hapless soul keeping house for a widower and his family in a back-country district of Norway. Bjørn still loves his dead wife, but he sees himself as 'a strong, healthy man with passions' (ibid., p. 181), drawn physically even to the woman who keeps his house, whom he considers an 'affected old chatterbox' (ibid., p. 181). Just as Sigrid Undset lets old Møller escape being trapped by his pity for Selma Brøter, Bjørn evades the demands of his physical nature with Miss Smith-Tellefsen only to fall victim to his predatory cousin Karen, one of Sigrid Undset's humorous caricatures, who soon after their marriage sends the housekeeper packing. Miss Smith-Tellefsen then becomes a 'paid companion', bereft of her meagre status as Bjørn's housekeeper, torn from the baby she had mothered, and, worst of all, denied any hope for the future. Her feeble attempt at socialising earns her a reprimand from her new employer that breaks her: 'She hardly knew why she felt so hopelessly poor and humiliated and forsaken, or why she wept so despairingly in her room' (ibid., p. 196).

The most powerful piece in the collection *Four Stories* is 'Simonsen' (1912), one of the few early stories Sigrid Undset wrote from the male point of view. Even here, however, the most poignant moments belong to Olga, a poor dressmaker who lives with Simonsen, an ageing labourer continually out of work, and their small daughter Svanhild. Despite his occasional binges, Simonsen is genuinely devoted to Olga and the child; he is tender, generous and loving, completely at the mercy of his mercenary son and his overbearing daughter-in-law, who have found him what few jobs he has had, probably the reason he has never been able to keep one. On Christmas Day, newly laid off and penniless after buying presents, Simonsen has to choose between marrying Olga and taking the new job his son has found, designed to put Simonsen out of their affairs for good. Simonsen leaves Olga and Svanhild, but '[for] a moment the wrongness of it struck a spark inside him and smarted and burned through all that life had left of Anton Simonsen's heart' (ibid., p. 245). As with Selma Brøter, Sigrid Undset hints at a providence responsible for both man's misery and his salvation; as old Simonsen wipes his eyes, he thinks: 'There must be One Above who decided these things. That must be his consolation: that there was One who decided . . .' (ibid., p. 246).

These stories indicate that Sigrid Undset was carrying on the realistic Scandinavian literary tradition begun in 1871, when Georg Brandes called for literature to demonstrate its vitality by submitting social problems to debate. Although she was dealing with some of the most downtrodden members of society, Sigrid Undset did not follow the Zolaesque trend then fashionable, attributing the chief responsibility for man's misery to his environment, heredity or the economic pressures he had to face. 'Simonsen', in particular, demonstrates Sigrid Undset's growing conviction that the individual is responsible for his fate, and that by making the right choice, no matter how painful, he may salvage some self-respect, if nothing more — or less. The moral sense that the characters of these stories possess also increasingly relates to their perception, however dim, of the hand of a God; Beate and Stener 'perhaps' see a supernatural design in Selma's fate, but Simonsen recognises that a God who makes decisions that man cannot make 'must' exist.

Jenny is the only one of Sigrid Undset's protagonists who runs away, unable to face the pain of life without her child. Even the poorest souls of these early short stories, however, draw strength from the bond between parent and child, which Sigrid Undset believed was essential to human life. Curiously enough, the men in 'Poor Fortunes' seem better endowed than the women with insight into basic human motivations, especially the physical needs through which women find their spiritual fulfilment in motherhood, a comment on the position of women in Western society. Sigrid Undset expanded on this theme in a significant essay, 'Some Reflections on the Suffragette Movement', which she sent to the Norwegian paper *Samtiden* in the latter part of 1912, when she was expecting her first child.

The notion of female suffrage had begun in England with the Chartist Movement in 1838–48, but legislative attempts to win English and American women the right to vote continued to fail, and in 1903 militant British suffragettes led by Emmeline Pankhurst and her daughters began a campaign of civil disobedience that continued until the outbreak of the First World War. Norway and Finland gave women limited suffrage in 1906 and 1907 respectively, and in 1913 Norwegian women became the first in Europe to receive full voting rights.

Writing in 1912, Sigrid Undset acknowledged 'how often these women [the suffragettes] have voluntarily undergone the bitterest martyrdom a woman can ever suffer — the martyrdom of ridicule' (quoted in Winsnes, *Sigrid Undset*, p. 63), and she felt that modern technology had changed women's position in society forever. She saw that women now could make their own decisions, rather than being forced into marriages merely to escape from responsibility, but she also believed that the feminist movement defied nature by attempting 'to make the unmarried self-sufficient career woman its norm and ideal, and in that way reduce woman's standing in life's most fundamental aspect . . . her position as wife and mother' (quoted in ibid., p. 63). Throughout her life Sigrid Undset vigorously opposed the notion of female self-sufficiency, which she felt threatened civilisation. During her first pregnancy, she idealistically observed, '. . . a woman can become nothing better than a good mother, and nothing much worse than a bad one' (quoted ibid., p. 63).

In December 1912, Sigrid Undset and Svarstad moved back to the same flat in the Via Fratina in Rome where they had met on Christmas Day 1909; now it was dank and cold, with snow blowing through the terrace door, and when Anders, their first child, was born there in January 1913 he was sickly. When the warm Roman spring only made his health more precarious, Sigrid Undset followed her doctor's advice and took the baby to her mother's home in Oslo. After Svarstad joined them, she rented two first-floor rooms at Ski, a half an hour's journey from Oslo. Svarstad had a studio in the city and commuted daily on a rickety milk train, a circumstance that must have diminished their companionship considerably.

At thirty-one, Sigrid Undset's artistic eye was turned on her first real home. Nini Roll Anker recalled that at Ski '[there] was not much furniture, but every piece was beautiful and most of it was old . . . her feeling for line and form is exceptionally sure and true . . .' (quoted in ibid., p. 60). For the rest of her life, Sigrid Undset preferred to wear the traditional Norwegian costume at home, and Mrs Anker's description of her as a young mother recalls Kristin Lavransdatter as the mistress of Husaby: 'When she presided over the white table-cloth in the panelled living-room . . . her hair plaited . . . in big bright braids . . . she had a tranquillity and dignity which always reminded me of the household mistresses of times long past' (ibid., p. 60).

While she was in Italy, Sigrid Undset had been working on 'The Fourth Commandment', an address she delivered in March 1914 to the Oslo Students' Union. Amid the international tension that led to the First World War, she traced all that was best in civilisation to the individual's sense of duty, his willingness 'to sacrifice his own life for the sake of another greater life' (quoted in ibid., p. 63). She voiced a stern moral idealism drawn from her wide reading and her humanistic orientation that was still not quite an orthodox expression of Christian belief; Carl Bayerschmidt has observed that at this time the God of Sigrid Undset's 'Fourth Commandment' was 'a symbol, though not the source of all good' (Bayerschmidt, *Sigrid Undset*, p. 32).

To Sigrid Undset as a new parent, the Fourth Commandment's injunction to children to honour their mothers and fathers also imposed the obligation for parents to do everything, sacrifice everything, in order to be worthy of their children's reverence. She felt that this loyalty was the only force holding civilisation together and allowing it to advance, a stern position that resembles the Old Germanic code of the *comitatus*, in which chieftain and warrior pledged mutual loyalty even unto death.

Culture, Sigrid Undset also believed, involved increasing responsibility toward one's fellow man, a duty, she claimed, to 'the inheritance which has been left to all humanity', and loyalty in its most extreme form was the common denominator of the noble products of civilisation she cited, placing the heroic defence of Thermopylae and 'the Catholic legends of the saints' side by side (quoted in Winsnes, *Sigrid Undset*, p. 64).

What mattered most to Sigrid Undset at this time was not the scope of the selfless act but its intent; not even its result, but man's inner strength to pursue virtues she thought people needed to learn: 'strength, wisdom, justice, truth, compassion, chastity, moderation, courage', all 'bright and ancient words' she said in her 1914 address, 'which are halfway to becoming ridiculous' (quoted in ibid., p. 64).

Sigrid Undset's illustration of the virtue she considered most praiseworthy brightly illuminates her own moral certainty and the uncompromising ideals she presented in her fiction: she called Shakespeare's Brutus 'the noblest figure in all literature' (quoted in ibid., p. 65) — Brutus, who loved Julius Caesar as his father and murdered him for the ideal of Roman freedom. Most readers believe that at Philippi Brutus recognised his tragedy, that he had risked all and lost; but Sigrid Undset believed he won, calling Brutus 'the finest thought ever to enter a man's mind':

> — Countrymen,
> My heart doth joy that yet in all my life
> I found no man but he was true to me.
> *Julius Caesar, V, v, 33–5*

For Sigrid Undset, Brutus triumphed in his intellectual chastity; 'love for everything immaculate and steadfast . . . disloyalty, which is for him the ugliest sin, has never come near him' (quoted in Winsnes, *Sigrid Undset*, p. 65). Sigrid Undset realised that Brutus' nobility belonged to art, not life, but in the close of her address on the Fourth Commandment she came full circle to parent and child, calling for ordinary human beings 'to wither into the truth', as Joyce put it, with age. For Sigrid Undset: 'The wisdom of age and the goodness of age are rare. . . . They are the same qualities as those we have had to attribute to God. . . . To gain [them] for himself is the best that any man can do for his child' (ibid., p. 67).

In May 1914, Svarstad went to Paris. Sigrid Undset joined him there, but cut her visit short because she was uneasy about Anders, whom she had left with her mother in Oslo. Nevertheless, in autumn of the same year Sigrid Undset stayed alone at Anne Kures' boarding house to write her next novel, *Vaaren* ('Spring'), without interruptions (Krane, *Sigrid Undset*, p. 43). Although the relationship of a woman to her family is, appropriately enough, its central theme, some critics feel that this novel lacks the quality of her other work.

Vaaren ('Spring')

Sigrid Undset completed her fourth novel in November 1914, fictionalising her theories on life and love and making her protagonists, Torkild and Rose, work out their marriage by compromising with each other's ideals. Torkild, from a miserable broken home, yearns for the kind of happiness Rose received from her loving mother, a glowing portrait of Charlotte Undset, who in the face of her poverty maintained an abundantly cultured family life. Despite her background, or because of its spiritual support, Rose has longed for a man who could 'tear her out of herself' (quoted in Winsnes, *Sigrid Undset*, p. 70), someone who could change her completely, and once they are married she finds Torkild, whom she has known 'forever', as comfortable and undemanding as an old shoe. For his part, he realises that Rose's self-centredness had needed the ideal husband they both know he is not. After their child is stillborn, Torkild refuses to have another because he senses Rose had accepted him only out of loneliness. They are finally reconciled, however, by abandoning their hopeless expectations, Sigrid Undset's definition of maturity.

'Spring' is essentially a social novel focused on the institution of the home, which Sigrid Undset believed was the building block of society. In this novel, written midway in her own marriage, she had arrived at a traditionally Christian solution to marital problems: Torkild had to accept Rose's conviction that she 'was not created to be married without children' (quoted in Bayerschmidt, *Sigrid Undset*, p. 80), and, for her part, Rose had to live with the consequences of his declaration that: '. . . no man can live his own life without reaching out into the lives of others' (ibid., p. 79).

After the outbreak of the First World War in August 1914, Sigrid Undset also adapted Malory's *Le Morte Darthur* as *Fortellinger om Kong Artur og ridderne av det runde bord* ('Tales of King Arthur and the Knights of the Round Table'. Since the time of Magnus Law-mender in the thirteenth century, the Arthurian legends had been Norway's most cherished chivalric romances, and Malory was one of Sigrid Undset's favourite authors. As one Norwegian who despite her country's official neutrality could not be silent in 1914, she used her version of *Le Morte Darthur* to proclaim Christianity's crusade against the Saxon hordes of northern Germany. For her, Arthur's saga was further proof that while manners and customs might change from century to century, '. . . the human heart alters not a whit through all the days' (quoted in Winsnes, *Sigrid Undset*, p. 86). Sigrid Undset could not help celebrating England's defence of its faith, which seemed to her as real in the twentieth century as it had in the old days when, at the Battle of Maldon, hearth-warriors, obedient to their oath, died to a man defending the body of an English earl slain by heathen Vikings.

As the war continued remorselessly and Europe's concept of chivalry perished in the trenches, Sigrid Undset herself sustained one of the most devastating blows a mother can face. Her daughter Maren Charlotte, whom the family affectionately called 'Tulla' and 'Mosse', was born in 1915, epileptic and severely retarded. Charlotte Blindheim recalls that until Tulla's death in 1939, Sigrid Undset's life centred upon her daughter. 'She was the one of the children who most resembled her mother, lovely and gentle and always beautifully dressed. "Tulla has never caused me an hour's grief", said Moster Sigrid . . . she never stopped missing her'.[6]

Nini Roll Anker called the three years beginning in 1916, when Sigrid Undset moved from Ski to Sinsen in Oslo's East Aker district, the most difficult time in her friend's life (Bayerschmidt, *Sigrid Undset*, p. 33). Following his divorce, Svarstad's first wife Ragna Moe had had to go to work at a menial job, and she had to put their three children in an orphanage because she could not support them (Krane, *Sigrid Undset*, p. 45). From the start, Sigrid Undset wanted a good relationship with them, and she took them under her own roof at Sinsen, caring for them just as she did Anders and Tulla and her third child Hans, born in 1919. She later commented: 'A painter's income in Norway will scarcely ever be sufficient to bring up a family of six, especially as two of the children, my stepson and my daughter, were mental cases'. During the First World War, when prices were high and goods were scarce, Sigrid Undset said she 'wrote books, kept house, and took care of the children' (*Twentieth Century Authors*, p. 1,433), a laconic description for a gruelling test of her devotion to what she considered her duty. She was a woman of strong constitution, accustomed to eighteen-hour working days, but she was in her mid-thirties and her pregnancies had been close together. She coped with her difficult financial situation by writing, and even if she did not succeed in overcoming her day-to-day problems completely, her fiction witnesses that she faced them with unfaltering courage and honesty.

Splinten av troldspeilet ('Images in a Mirror')

Sigrid Undset's next book appeared in 1917, titled *Splinten av troldspeilet*, literally 'Splinter from the Troll's Looking-Glass', an allusion to Hans Christian Andersen's tale in which people see a distorted world through a magic mirror. The title also has Christian overtones in its hint at the Biblical parable of the mote in one's neighbour's and the beam in one's own eye. *Splinten av troldspeilet* contains two complementary views of marriage, the novellas 'Fru Waage' and 'Fru Hjelde', but only the latter has been published in English.[7]

Harriet Waage and Uni Hjelde occupy adjoining apartments in the same down-at-heel Oslo town-house, mirror-image reflections of modern marriage. Bayerschmidt observes a close thematic relation between these stories and 'Spring', though he points out that the novel 'is written from the standpoint of both husband and wife, who must share equally in ... [marital] responsibilities ... whereas *Images in a Mirror* [he refers to the original] is written from the woman's point of view ... focused directly on ... Uni Hjelde and Harriet Waage' (*Sigrid Undset*, p. 81).

Harriet Waage's 'progressive' family background has given her no moral basis for dealing with a perfunctory marriage to her wealthy cousin Frederik Waage and his indifference when their young son is drowned; she turns for sympathy to a lover, Henning Damm. Uni Hjelde, who had appeared in Sigrid Undset's 1908 story 'The Happy Age', thinks Harriet fulfils the free-thinking desire to 'live for one's self alone', while Uni herself, as this story opens, is crushed beneath the burden of lower-middle-class motherhood. Five children in ten years, with her first son already dead, have brought her to the brink of collapse.

Uni's devoted husband Kristian finally arranges a holiday for her at a mountain *saeter*, where she regains her health and meets an old acquaintance, Vegard, who tempts her with the dream of the modest stage career she had given up. After Uni returns to Oslo she nearly begins an affair with Vegard, but at no time does she allow herself or Vegard to imagine that she loves him.

A selfless neighbour, Miss Bormann, shows Uni that she had seen too clearly the mote in her husband's eye — his immersion in his work and his lack of sensitivity to her renunciation of her acting career. Not until Uni is on the verge of meeting Vegard for an assignation, however, does she recognise the beam that is in her own: it is her concept of her artistic talent, 'a force that splits up and paralyses all one's capacity for living. It makes one . . . incapable of holding fast to any one line' (*Images in a Mirror*, pp. 221–2). Once she and Kristian remove the splinters from each other's eyes by sharing the emotions and dreams their commonplace lives had obscured for so long, Uni can see her duty plainly: 'And I can no more run away from my place than a solder can in battle' (ibid., p. 222).

In the other novella, Harriet Waage does try to run away, breaking up her own home and her lover Damm's, but she realises with bitterness that this marriage will be as empty as her first. She is blind to the well-meant advice of her cousin Dr Alice Falch, who urges Harriet to see the world in relation to God rather than to self. Alice represents the conservative Christian belief that one must do penance for a few moments of happiness, a view Sigrid Undset first pronounced through Uni, who at last saw the price of being *Mrs* Hjelde: '. . . how is it that I, at my age, can go on believing in happiness — or doubting it either . . . in the brief moment when love's caresses are new and make the blood flutter, you must understand and take control of all your life'. Happiness in her children, Uni now sees, is the only certainty of motherhood: 'As long as I have my children I know that I can go on living, and gladly too, no matter how everything else in life turns out for me' (ibid., p. 226).

De kloge jomfruer ('The Wise Virgins')

The title of Sigrid Undset's next collection of short stories, 'The Wise Virgins' (not translated), recalls a folk motif widely used in Norwegian *billedteppe*,[8] wall hangings woven to celebrate daughters' baptisms and taken with them to their new homes when they marry; Sigrid Undset's use of the term suggests a newly religious orientation in her work. If, as A.H. Winsnes maintains, Jenny's 'ideal of purity' sprang from her 'unconscious religious feelings' (*Sigrid Undset*, p. 54), the same ideal destroyed her, because she could not acknowledge her submission to a power greater than herself. Just before she opened her veins, Jenny claimed: 'I call nothing happiness if it's not the happiness I required. I still believe such happiness exists. If it does not exist for me, then it was I who failed, it was I who was a foolish virgin who could not watch and wait for the bridegroom . . .' (ibid., p. 54).

Sigrid Undset drew her 1918 'wise virgins' from Oslo's humble folk. 'Smaapiker' ('Little Girls'), is the story of two youngsters who, like their older counterparts, vie for a two-year-old boy's affection. Once close, the girls become jealous of one another when he chooses between them, ruining their friendship forever. 'Gunnvald og Emma' ('Gunnvald and Emma'), traces Emma's attempts to make her marriage to Gunnvald, a widower, succeed, despite difficulties with his children, old enough at their mother Klara's death to have been shaped by her attitude: 'Some women feel their sex as an impulse to live for someone else, but Klara was one of those who feel it as something which gives them the right to live on someone else' (quoted in Bayerschmidt, *Sigrid Undset*, p. 86). When Emma's own child arrives, however, Gunnvald for the first time grants her her human dignity.

The powerfully moving 'Thjodolf' (1918),[9] is the masterpiece of Sigrid Undset's first literary phase. In this story, Helene Johansen waits for a bridegroom but chooses one who proves unworthy, having neither the dance nor the house that the Biblical parable of the Wise and Foolish Virgins promised. All Helene receives from life is a pitiably short time with a foster child, Thjodolf, whose natural mother Fanny at first rejects him but later takes him back, only to return him to Helene after her dissolute living irremediably ruins the child's health. Helene loses not only the child but her irresponsible husband Julius too; at Thjodolf's funeral, Helene discovers that Julius is the father of the child Fanny is carrying. Not once does Sigrid Undset allow this parable of moral courage degenerate into sentimentality, preferring instead her objective 'Woman's Point of View' as she expressed it in one of her most famous essays, that 'the normal human being . . . has always had a central shrine, the fireside of his home, and from there he had kindled all his altar-fires' (quoted in Winsnes, *Sigrid Undset*, p. 75), attributing the human religious impulse to the central phenomenon of the family.

Although Sigrid Undset was reticent about her own marriage, these years must have placed serious pressures on her relationship with her husband. Borghild Krane believes that Sigrid

Undset's bitterness in later years stemmed from her realisation that Svarstad never offered the children any fatherly support, and that he was indeed incapable of being the family man she felt he should have been (*Sigrid Undset*, p. 49). In fairness, Svarstad must have felt like an outsider; he was not cut out for fatherhood, he did not fit into the artistic life in Oslo, and the literary circle that admired Sigrid Undset refused to accept him (ibid., p. 50). Some of her male characters, like Vegard, who tempts Uni Hjelde like 'a salesman in life's goods' (*Images in Mirror*, p. 224), and Julius, whose physical desires overcome his loyalty to his wife in 'Thjodolf', exhibit a devil-may-care egotism something like the early attraction Njal's son Skarphedin had had for Sigrid Undset when she was a girl, watching him throw his life away with a noble gesture. However magnetic such behaviour might have seemed, Sigrid Undset at this time could not reconcile it with what she considered the individual's primary duty — the home. She wrote to Nini Roll Anker: 'I have never believed in "sacred egotism", neither for artists nor for anyone else. Individualism, if by that we mean the right to demand special privileges for one's own individuality at the expense of others, merely makes it easier for power mentalities to subjugate others' (quoted in Bayer-schmidt, *Sigrid Undset*, p. 84).

During the First World War, Sigrid Undset seemed to be turning towards a spiritual, rather than a human, concept of a lord. In 1915, she had already written to Mrs Anker: '. . . the Church of Rome has at any rate form; it does not irritate the intelligence as do these diverse Protestant sects . . . something else we have to thank the Germans for . . . in my opinion *das Volk der Dichter und Denker* both write and think damned badly' (quoted in Winsnes, *Sigrid Undset*, p. 77). Sigrid Undset had disliked German 'power mentalities' for a long time, and when the 1918 Armistice closed their first attempt to dominate Europe, she became concerned with the 'so-called scientific outlook' she analysed in 1919 in three essays collectively titled *Et kvindesyns-punkt* ('A Woman's Point of View'). She wryly observed: 'I usually write articles when I am angry' (quoted in ibid., p. 81), and in one of these essays she swung a Viking battle-axe at 'half-learned and quarter-learned vagrants of science' who muddled 'spiritual, organic and mechanical phenomena', in par-ticular Kitti Anker Møller, whose pamphlet *A Birth-Policy for*

Women advocated turning children over to the state for cash. Sigrid Undset must have also inflamed countless feminist sensibilities by insisting: 'If one considers the fundamentally different positions in which the two sexes stand toward the child [they both created] all talk about equality between men and women becomes utter nonsense' (quoted in ibid., p. 84), a problem only now, some fifty years after her death, being widely discussed. In the essay 'Postscript' she carried the gist of her 'Fourth Commandment' address still further, claiming that Christianity's doctrine of the Virgin Mary 'has given to women the most honourable position they have as yet been assigned' (quoted in ibid., p. 84), and in 'Women and the World War' she also proclaimed that the Church in its broad sense 'has been the bearer of those ideals which cannot die — the majority of men do not succeed in living in accordance with them, but they always rediscover after a time that they cannot live without them' (quoted in ibid., p. 77).

With sad irony, at the same time that Sigrid Undset was beginning to realise she could not live without the ideal of Christ as her master, her marriage was dissolving. Borghild Krane claims that Sigrid Undset and Svarstad shared an 'uncompromising nature which exacerbated the clash of their differing talents and their differing temperaments. Neither remarried; neither lived an unconventional bohemian existence, even though Svarstad was less adapted for a bourgeois existence than Sigrid Undset wished to be' (*Sigrid Undset*, p. 51).

When she and Svarstad separated by mutual consent in July 1919, a month before the birth of her child Hans, their marriage ended in spirit, if not yet in fact. Sigrid Undset moved her family to Lillehammer, a small historic town at the southern end of the Gudbrandsdal, Norway's most beautiful valley, where she lived until the Nazis forced her into exile in 1940.

Notes

1. Stanley J. Kunitz and Howard Haycroft (eds.), *Twentieth Century Authors* (New York: H.W. Wilson, 1942; 7th Printing 1973), p. 1,433.
2. Quoted in A.H. Winsnes, *Sigrid Undset: A Study in Christian Realism*,

trans. P.G. Foote (New York: Sheed and Ward, 1953) p. 58.

3. Borghild Krane, *Sigrid Undset. Liv og meninger* (Oslo: Gyldendal, 1970), p. 39.

4. Carl Bayerschmidt, *Sigrid Undset* (New York: Twayne, 1970), p. 74.

5. 'Selma Brøter', 'Miss Smith-Tellefsen' and 'Simonsen', all originally published in 1912, are included with 'Thjodolf' (1918) in *Four Stories*, trans. Naomi Walford (New York: Knopf, 1959).

6. Charlotte Blindheim, *Moster Sigrid. Et familie portrett av Sigrid Undset* (Oslo: Aschehoug, 1982) p. 8. My translation.

7. In *Images in a Mirror*, trans. Arthur G. Chater(New York: Knopf, 1938).

8. I am grateful to Lila Hauge for this insight into traditional Norwegian tapestry motifs.

9. Included in *Four Stories*.

5 The Sins of the Fathers:
Kristin Lavransdatter 1919–24

What I have sinned — it is fit I must expiate.
Henrik Ibsen, *Rosmersholm*

In every sense that mattered to her — spiritually, artistically, most of all maternally — Sigrid Undset was building her permanent home during her first five years at Lillehammer. For a little more than a year after Hans' birth she rented a house there, but in late 1920 she bought an old farmhouse which its former owner had brought to Lillehammer from Sør-Fron. In 1924 she bought another that came from Sel in Gudbrandsdal. She connected the two buildings, filling and surrounding them with nearly four hundred varieties of plants, and, 'Just to irritate my Danish relatives', she joked, she named her home 'Bjerkebaek', a reference to a prototypically Norwegian stage character. She furnished her home with lovely old pieces out of Norway's past, and when she finished in 1924, only the piano and the plumbing were new. Charlotte Blindheim recalls: '. . . if it is true that a house can have a soul, it [Bjerkebaek] came to be considered more as "Home" than any other I have known. Every object was stamped with Moster Sigrid's highly personal taste . . . It was a wonderful place to be because it exuded the feeling that she liked to have us around, that we were welcome there, always, just as in our own home.'[1]

Creating this atmosphere singlehanded cannot have been easy for Sigrid Undset. The writing that supported her family had to be done late at night on black coffee and cigarettes, and even her strong constitution must have suffered. In the spiritual sense, however, her art saved her, for as she worked on *Kristin Lavransdatter* from 1919 to 1924, she was drawing closer to God.

By deliberately choosing rural Lillehammer over Oslo where she had spent most of her life, Sigrid Undset was also rededicating herself to Norway, not just its city life which she had already described so powerfully, but the history and culture she had grown to love as a child. Harald Beyer observes that the basic harmony of Norwegian literature springs from the triad of forest, sea, and mountains. Norway 'rises steeply from the sea . . . is cracked into narrow fjords and channels, which lead gradually into the "dark, church-still valleys", the desolate mountain wastes, the endless forests, and the open, smiling country'.[2] The harmony of her daily round at Lillehammer, one of Norway's loveliest natural settings, must have heightened Sigrid Undset's awareness of her Norwegian heritage, and at the same time, as she raised her eyes to the Dovre mountains beyond, her Creator must have seemed constantly near.

Lillehammer, an ancient town, lies on the north shore of Lake Mjøsa, Norway's largest lake, and on the Royal Road from Oslo to Trondheim (Nidaros), where Norway's kings still go to be crowned. Lillehammer is also 60 kilometres (about 37 miles) north-west of Hamar, where Nicholas Breakspear, later Pope Adrian IV, established his bishopric in 1152, the religious centre for the entire Gudbransdal area. Lillehammer is now a well-known resort town with a population of about 22,000, famous for Maihaugen, an outdoor museum exhibiting authentic homes, churches, and workshops of the Gudbrandsdal district. Begun in 1901 by Anders Sandvig, Maihaugen displays the Bjørnstad farm, twenty-six buildings grouped around two courtyards just as they had been in their original Gudbrandsdal location, and although this farm dates only from the seventeenth century, scholars believe it accurately represents Norse farmsteads of medieval times. Sigrid Undset may have used it in part as her model for Jörundgaard, where Kristin Lavransdatter grew up, setting Jörundgaard at the real-life Romungard, a farm up the valley 3 kilometres (1¾ miles) from Otta, near Sel, where part of Sigrid Undset's own home had come from, 1,000 feet above sea level and about 114 kilometres (72 miles) north of Lillehammer on the road to Trondheim. Near Romungard the valley narrows, climbing into the Dovre plateau which contains Norway's highest mountain, the 8,104-foot Glittertind, and passing through Hjerkinn, a 3,000-foot mountain hospice for pilgrims like Kristin Lavransdatter on their way to St Olav's shrine at Nidaros. The saint's tomb had given rise to Nidaros Cathedral. the first stone structure in Norway, built between 1066 and 1093. Rebuilt four times after its first fire in 1328, the cathedral at Trondheim remains the spiritual heart of Norway.

The Trøndelag district, where Kristin Lavransdatter came as

mistress of Erland Nikulausson's manor at Husaby and where she died of plague at the convent of Rein, lies 170 kilometres (105 miles) north-west of Otta, on Norway's extreme west coast, only three degrees from the Arctic Circle. It contains about 10 per cent of Norway's present population, about 15 per cent of its tilled land, and 14 per cent of its forest. The ice-free Trondheimsfjord thrives as ever, supplying oil year-round to Scandinavian ports closed in winter, when once it welcomed its hardy Trönder shipmen home from trading voyages and Viking forays to England and the Continent; the folk of Trøndelag had reacted strongly against Olav Tryggvasson's ferocious attempt to impose Christianity upon them between 970 and 990, and the area maintained its pagan religion and its warrior values considerably longer than the rest of Norway did. Sigrid Undset knew Trondheim and its surrounding farmland well from her summers with her father's pious hardworking family, and she purposely chose it as the goal of Kristin Lavransdatter's journey through life.

Although she had not written about medieval Norway since *Gunnar's Daughter* in 1909, Sigrid Undset had been carrying on formidable research into the period, especially the question of Norway's relationship to the rest of Europe. Both A.H. Winsnes and Carl Bayerschmidt point out that between 1900 and 1920, Norwegians in general were taking an extraordinary interest in the Middle Ages. European Romantic writers had already 'discovered' the Middle Ages, calling them the birth of the European community and acknowledging the twelfth and thirteenth centuries as 'one of the great creative epochs' but German 'racial romanticism ... [had] excluded the northern lands from Europe',[3] a theory which when later exaggerated lent pseudo-mystical momentum to the Nazi movement. Norway's writers did, however, differ radically from the German Romantics; Harald Beyer observes that in a country that looks, as Bjørnson put it, 'toward the eternal snows', writers only rarely can 'cultivate the blue flower of beauty, the art for art's sake' (*A History*, p. 5) that Novalis romantically advanced as literature's goal. Nineteenth-century Scandinavian scholars were of two minds about Norway's artistic relationship to the rest of Europe; most saw their lands as outside Europe's common civilisation, with some believing that their late Christian conversion had only scratched the surface of the Scandinavian character, and others convinced that Christianity had fatally debilitated the noble Viking spirit by insisting on humility and forgiveness. Edvard Bull, who Beyer claims held 'a more or less Marxist view' in the 1920s (ibid., p. 316), maintained in *Nation and Church in the Middle Ages* that 'it would have been a task for other men than the priests of the eleventh, twelfth and thirteenth centuries, to teach self-sufficient and independent Norwegian farmers that they were sinful mortals, who before everything else had need of grace and redemption' (quoted in Winsnes, *Sigrid Undset*, p. 99).

Scandinavians began to perceive their role in Europe's cultural evolution differently when interest in the sociological aspects of archaeology awakened in the 1870s and 1880s, during Ingvald Undset's short-lived career. Fredrik Paasche, whom Sigrid Undset respected deeply, used the then little-known body of Old Norse Christian literature, mainly translations of Latin originals, to demonstrate that '. . . it was contact with Europe and the acquisition of Christian civilization that made the greatest impact on the culture of medieval Norway'.[4] By citing the Christian elements in skaldic poems and the power of Christian religious verse, Paasche believed that 'the creative and constructive will towards peace and order, the desire for the beautiful and the spiritual elevation of existence — aspirations liberated by Christianity . . . [mark] the greatest effort of the Norwegian medieval period' (quoted in Winsnes, *Sigrid Undset*, p. 100).

Sigrid Undset exercised her 'living memories' of earlier ages most fully in her two medieval novels, but other work she produced between 1919 and 1924 besides *Kristin Lavransdatter*, notably her essay 'Om folkviser' ('On Ballads', not translated), 1921, and her 1923 translations of three Icelandic sagas, indicate that she steeped herself thoroughly in Norse folklore and the saga style which plays such an important role in *Kristin Lavransdatter*. Paasche also called her attention to the *Diplomatarium Norvegicum*, a compendium of laws, documents, and letters that became her most important source of medieval material; she felt it unequivocally supported her conviction that 'the Christian evaluation of life had struck deeper roots in Norway than in the other Scandinavian countries' (ibid., p. 103).

Kristin Lavransdatter comprises three novels: *The Bridal Wreath*, 1920; *The Mistress of Husaby*, 1921; and *The Cross*, 1922. Because Sigrid Undset set her major medieval novels in relatively little-documented historical periods, she allowed herself freedom to concentrate on her character's inner lives. Bayerschmidt has also noted that 'Sigrid Undset never cared to draw any sharp line between past and present' (*Sigrid Undset*, p. 90), an indication that she knew that she was dealing with eternal verities of human existence, matters D.H. Lawrence claimed could only be conveyed in mythic form, because 'they lie too deep in the blood and soul, for mental explanation or description'.[5]

Kristin Lavransdatter opens in 1306, at a time when saga writing was dwindling, the power of the old warrior aristocracy was fading under the restrictive laws Magnus Law-mender had instituted a generation earlier, and Norway was becoming helplessly impoverished by both Hanseatic economic supremacy and Swedish expansionism. On the death of Haakon V in 1319, Magnus VII, the three-year-old son of Haakon's daughter Lady Ingebjørg, assumed the thrones of Norway and his murdered father Duke Erik's Sweden through the efforts of Erik's Danish vassal Knut Porse, who later married Ingebjørg. After reaching his majority, Magnus largely ignored Norway, leaving the country without a lawful government in 1333, when a party of Norwegian nobles led by Sir Erling Vidkunsson, who had been Magnus' Norwegian regent, rose briefly and without onus against the King. Norwegian farmers and chieftains had always maintained that a king who tried to rule unlawfully could be set aside, and Sigrid Undset used that traditional right to justify a fictional attempt by Erlend Nikulausson, Kristin's charismatic husband, to separate the Crowns of Norway and Sweden and place Ingebjørg's older son by Knut Porse on the Norwegian throne. Erlend failed, but the risk was well worth it; had he been succeessful, Norway might have had lasting peace and their ancient laws and customs might have been upheld. Instead, the country slipped into disaster, scourged by the Black Death and relegated to inferiority in its union with Denmark and Sweden in 1397.

The Bridal Wreath (1920)

In *The Bridal Wreath*, the first and most lyrical volume of *Kristin Lavransdatter*, Sigrid Undset follows her heroine from childhood to marriage in a succession of betrayals — a price that her own life had taught her was the cost of growing up. Magnus Law-mender's reforms have caused irreversable changes in Norwegian society; both Lavrans Björgulfsson and his wife Ragnfrid come from noble stock, Lavrans having served with distinction in the bodyguard of King Haakon Magnusson, but by the time Kristin, their first surviving child, is a few years old, they have settled into farming at Jörundgaard in Gudbrandsdal, where for his wife's sake Lavrans has moved from his estate near Oslo. Ragnfrid's invariably sombre mood is one of the few shadows at Jörundgaard, which under Lavrans' management represents all that is good in Norwegian husbandry. One day Lavrans takes little Kristin to visit one of his *saeters*, a mountain pasturage where she experiences the first frightening wrench of maturity from which not even Lavrans' loving strength can shield her; she wanders into the woods with his red stallion Guldsveinen, ad-mires her own reflection in a forest pool, and glimpses 'a fairy lady' who holds out a wreath of golden flowers, the traditional symbol of maidenhood Scandinavian brides wear as a symbol of their family's honour. Although a little later the saintly Brother Edvin offers Kristin a different garland, the promise of eternal bliss as a bride of Christ, she rejects it for the wreath of worldly gold representing her own will and desire, a selfishness that constantly tempts Kristin Lavransdatter into the betrayals of trust that shape her life.

Ragnfrid, often preoccupied with her grief at the loss of three sons and the care of Kristin's paralysed little sister Ulvhild, and Lavrans, the most tolerant of fathers, allow Kristin to mingle freely with their servants' children. By the time they are adoles-cents, Arne, a boy like Olav, Sigrid Undset's young friend from Drøbak, hopelessly adores Kristin and begs her to meet him secretly the night before he leaves to take service at another manor. After an hour or two of the first innocent 'lad and girl' tenderness Kristin had ever known, they part, but on her way home Kristin is assaulted by another man, leaving her violated in spirit, though not in body.

Kristin hides the attack from her parents, and soon afterwards Arne dies in a brawl with her attacker; his mother accuses Kristin of causing his death. Lavrans decides to betroth her at the customary age of fifteen to Simon Andresson, a respectable farmer of good family whose lands adjoin his own, but Kristin begs her father to send her to a convent near Oslo for a year before the wedding. There she meets a man like no other she has ever known, the dashing Erlend Nikulausson, second cousin to the King, thirteen years older than Kristin and at that time attempting to extricate himself from an unsavoury affair with Eline Ormsdatter, a married woman who had borne him two children. Passion's lightning strikes Kristin and Erlend at once and they swear their faith to one another, flouting their earlier obligations; together they became involved in Eline's death, and Kristin's will at last overcomes Lavrans' scruples, forcing her father to break his word of betrothal to Simon and give her in marriage to Erlend, who is everything Lavrans would never be. Sick with loss but as yet unaware that Kristin is bearing Erlend's child, Lavrans confesses his own sin to Ragnfrid on his daughter's wedding night, how he had come into his own marriage loveless; for her part, Ragnfrid reveals that she had married Lavrans after giving herself to another man. These hidden sins have galled them both like horsehair shirts, making their outwardly blameless life as Christian man and wife as ignoble a sham as the crown of maidenhood Kristin's fatal pride had turned to fool's gold.

In Norwegian literature, the forest often represents the mystical element of life, hiding both secret solace and supernatural terrors. Human sexuality, that ennobling and bedevilling mystery of life, burns deep within *Kristin Lavransdatter* and its eponymous heroine. In this novel Sigrid Undset probes the bonds of loyalty demanded by love and the agony that results when they are broken. *The Bridal Wreath* begins as every child does, in an innocent Eden, but Kristin's headlong pursuit of knowledge in its Biblical as well as its experiential sense ruptures the illusory peace, flawed by his own failure to love, that Lavrans had created at Jörundgaard.

No one Kristin loves on earth can live happily ever after, least of all herself and the man she swore to love in that one bright moment when, like Uni Hjelde, all unknowing, she had to decide the course of her life. When she chooses to disobey her father and become a woman in Erlend's arms, Kristin shatters *The Bridal Wreath*'s fairy-tale atmosphere, every young girl's dream, and traps herself in the dark woods of the unconscious that lure the unwary with promises of sensual delight; but the bitterest betrayals Kristin's desire forces her to make prove to be the ones she inflicts on herself.

The Mistress of Husaby (1921)

In contrast to the poignantly lyric *Bridal Wreath*, *The Mistress of Husaby* is an epic novel centred on Kristin Lavransdatter's failure to recognise and understand the needs of the man she has chosen as her lord. At the beginning of this volume of her manuscript, Sigrid Undset wrote: 'In memory of my father Ingvald Undset' (Bayerschmidt, *Sigrid Undset*, p. 161), an indication of the tribute she paid him in the figure of Lavrans Björgulfsson. Like many of Sigrid Undset's titles, *The Mistress of Husaby*, referring to Erlend Nikulausson's ancestral manor twenty miles south-west of Nidaros in the Trøndelag, proves ironic from the moment Kristin arrives, pregnant and drained by seasickness, in its great knights' hall. Husaby lives by customs far older and nobler than Jörundgaard's; it has descended to Erlend from his great-aunt's father, Earl Skule, Snorri Sturlusson's friend and patron, whom the warrior aristocracy of Norway made king before he fell to the low-born *Birkebeiner* in 1240 — the great days of medieval Norway when the sagas were being written and pagan and Christian ideals met and clashed.

Kristin's attention passes over the weaponry that adorns Husaby's walls, even over Erlend's sword and his white shield with its red lion rampant, St Olaf's royal emblem of Norway, symbols of Erlend's honour fastened as was the custom behind the high seat to which he had brought her. All she can see are unwashed walls black with dirt and soot behind the priceless tapestries, lice creeping through the linen sheets of her bridal bed and signs of mismanagement accusing Erlend — and herself — from every corner of the neglected manor. Rapidly losing her tender dream of love in obsessive housewifery and tormented by her secret knowledge that she has wounded her father far more grievously by her pregnancy than Lavrans yet knows, Kristin hurls herself into protracted domesticity broken only by the harrowing birth of her first son. She and Erlend then realise that nothing can ever be the same for them again.

Both seek forgiveness after their fashion. Erlend travels alone in midwinter on skis to Jörundgaard, braving weather and wolves to face a worse ordeal, to present Lavrans Björgulfsson with the shameful news of a grandchild born too soon. The next spring Kristin walks barefoot the twenty miles to St Olaf's shrine at

71

Nidaros. Erlend's penance is successful because he makes it, as he does everything, with all his heart, and as Lavrans returns with him to Husaby, Lavrans discovers he likes Erlend better than he wished he did; the two men Kristin loves strike up a lasting connection. In contrast, Kristin's penance proves sadly spurious, for in bearing son after son her savage maternal devotion injures her father still more as he lies dying, and finally drives Erlend from her.

Galled by inactivity, Erlend accepts the offer of the young King's regent, Sir Erling Vidkunsson, to take ship and defend Norway's remote north coast from the Russians. Erlend becomes Captain of the Vargoy stronghold and Keeper of the Northern Marches for two years, so successfully that he receives 'the cure for his honour that he had wished for all these years — to be given the Wardenship his father had once held'[6] of Orkdola, a vindication, Erlend believes, of his warrior's skills for which the new stay-at-home lords of Norway resent him so deeply.

When young King Magnus puts Sweden's interests before Norway's, however, Erlend throws himself into a conspiracy to put Lady Ingebjørg's older son on the Norwegian throne, separating the kingdoms. Through his own indiscretion the plot is discovered and Erlend is imprisoned. Although he is tortured, he never reveals the names of those he swore to the enterprise; in the custom of older days, on the hilt of his sword, a sword which bore the runes, 'Keep thy troth'. Erlend loses his lands and most of his possessions, and emerges with little but his life; he even has to bear the knowledge that Simon, from whom he had taken Kristin, has had to sue for his release. Despite it all, Erlend leaves his prison 'like a chieftain parting from the housefolk at a wedding-feast' (*The Mistress of Husaby*, p. 138).

Norwegian writers often symbolise a longing for adventure, beauty, and freedom with the open sea, the whale's high road that liberates, purifies and endlessly fascinates the restless masculine soul. Shut out of Kristin's love by her relentless maternity, Erlend feels his spirit rusting like an unused sword, and he longs for the security of a stout deck beneath his feet and the sword's values that he knew, rather than the housebound responsibilities for which, like Anders Svarstad, he had little experience and less inclination.

Erlend Nikulausson is a chieftain of the old order, the kind

Sigrid Undset described in her *Saga of Saints*: 'If a man fought on in spite of it [destiny] he won the only things a man *can* [italics in original] win: honor and fame. This could nerve the highborn chieftain to great deeds: his life was worth high stakes' (ibid., p. 150). Erlend knew his men as they knew him, and he saw Norway's decline clearly: '"these stubborn Trönders liked us great folk better in the old days when we led their sons to battle and foray, let our blood flow out over the deck-planks mixed with theirs, and hewed rings in sunder and shared the booty with our housecarls"' (ibid., p. 129). All too often the soldier's skills are not needed or appreciated in peacetime, and farmers too easily forget that the warrior pays his tithes in blood. Kristin fails tragically to see that Erlend will never willingly violate a trust placed wholeheartedly in him, while she allows her smothering love for her children and her fruitless labour for Husaby to come between them, refusing to acknowledge his innate nobility of spirit and blaming him for his inability to be what he is not — a man like Lavrans. Kristin, not Erlend, violates the spirit, if not the letter, of the promise she made to him when they first loved: '"May God forsake me if I take any other man to my arms so long as I live on earth"'.[7]

The Cross (1922)

Sigrid Undset built Kristin Lavransdatter's *Cross* out of a sad succession of goodbyes, an elegy not so much for what was or what had to be, but like all the deepest human sorrows, for what might have been. King and archbishop divide Erlend's holdings, forcing him to live at Jörundgaard, which Lavrans had bequeathed to Kristin, among folk who resented 'this haughty Trönder chieftain' for dragging the best of their own into his abortive conspiracy. Erlend fills his empty days by hunting with his unruly sons, now chafing at their mother's overprotectiveness, while Kristin and Ulf, Erlend's kinsman and close comrade, struggle to keep Jörundgaard solvent in the teeth of poor crops and the ill-will of its dependents, who refuse to excuse either Ulf's foreign ways or Kristin's old sins against her parents. The same hardheartedness overwhelms Kristin's resolution not to blame Erlend for their plight as she watches her sons turning to him, preparing to fly from the nest she was slaving to preserve for them.

One measure of a man is his behaviour under adversity, when most people perversely find it easier to curse a benefactor than to hate an enemy. The young son of Simon, who had married Kristin's youngest sister Ramborg, falls deathly ill, and Kristin grimly repays Simon for Erlend's release by healing the boy with a pagan rite she had learned from Erlend's aunt, Lady Aashild, but all the while Kristin refuses to forgive Simon for risking his own reputation to save Erlend's life.

Simon himself finds that '[to] be forgiven by a man you have wronged can impose an intolerable strain'. Simon had only helped Erlend because despite everything Simon still loved Kristin. When Simon himself kills a man in a tavern for insulting Lavrans' memory, Erlend's quick wits and flashing sword save him. For the first time Simon sees Erlend Nikulausson at swordplay and recognises Kristin's husband not only as the warrior but also the man he knew he could never be himself.

Simon lacks Erlend's magnanimity; when Erlend casually reveals that he knows Simon still loves Kristin, Simon turns on him and severs the relationship between their families. Later, after Kristin flings at Erlend the one blow he cannot withstand, that she thinks him unfit to occupy Lavrans' high seat at Jörundgaard, Erlend leaves her and goes to the only land he still owns, the miserable little mountain farm at Haugen, said to be haunted by the ghosts of Lady Aashild and her husband who had killed her and then himself, unable to bear the knowledge that she had ruined herself by marrying him for love. When Simon tries to mend matters with Kristin, he is stricken by blood poisoning; before he dies he asks her to reconcile herself with Erlend, but Kristin again fulfils only the letter of the law, going to Haugen but refusing to stay where Erlend could be his own man.

The child Kristin bears from that failed reconciliation lives only a little while, and rumours fly that Ulf Haldorsson, not Erlend, was its father. When Erlend rushes to defend her, he is fatally wounded in a swift foolish clash with the farm folk who accuse her of adultery. Erlend dies with the smile of a fate-defying Norse chieftain on his lips, but not even then can Kristin forgive him for the pain she still does not see that she has caused for herself. Not until her youngest son has died and the older ones have taken up their own lives in monastery, farm and sword-service, and one, Gaute, has brought a clever, manipulating young wife to run Jörundgaard in her place, does Kristin Lavransdatter begin to ponder the meaning of her life. She takes the long pilgrim's road to Nidaros, this time walking in sincere penance with the poor and the sick, and settles at the Rein convent in the Trondheimsfjord. At the very end, with Ulf beside her once more, she sacrifices her life for a poor woman and herself succumbs to the plague. In her last possible chance for repentance, Kristin Lavransdatter glimpses the glorious light that Erlend's forgiveness had set before her; the path to Nidaros had been her Royal Road, because when she gives the Church the heavy gold ring set with a red stone by which Erlend had marked her as his wife, she suddenly sees that it had also set her apart with the red glow of martyrdom for her Lord and her God.

When she sets out on the last stage of her journey to Nidaros, Kristin's heart throbs at her last sight of home, Erlend's Haugen, 'high on the topmost mountain ridge'. Harald Beyer remarks that '[a] literature that has grown up among mountains may lack luxuriance and light-hearted gaiety, but it has the advantage of seriousness and greater perspective' ('Sigrid Undset', p. 4). Often, as in Ibsen's works, the mountains in Norway's literature symbolise artistic freedom in the self-disciplinary sense that the Hebrew prophets climbed Sinai to talk with God. The symbolic mountains Kristin Lavransdatter had to cross to her salvation were her soul-threatening betrayals of her parents, her husband, and herself, but at last when she gives her life for one of His people, she touches the face of God.

Every generation responds differently to those few great novels that offer many levels of meaning, and *Kristin Lavransdatter* has been read in differing ways: as an absorbing humanistic parable of man's journey from lyric youth through epic maturity to elegiac old age, or as a religious allegory in the mode of Scandinavian realism that traces the soul's path from the dark woods of sin through the purgatory of a valley of sea-salt tears to a mountain-top vision of God in Heaven. The story of Kristin and Erlend Nikulausson also portrays the archetypal biological snare where women must nurture in security and men must seek adventure, and in yet a deeper sense, both define themselves heroically by snatching victory out of defeat, choosing the quality of their conduct in the mythic sense, living forever beyond the restrictions of ordinary time.

In the context of human loyalty, a virtue cherished in both the Old Norse and the Christian beliefs, *Kristin Lavransdatter* encompasses mighty themes: the individual's search for God; the riddle of human sexuality; Norway's societal shift from a pagan warrior aristocracy to a feudal Christian culture, and the nation's decline from independence to subjection under Denmark and Sweden. A universal message also appears in Sigrid Undset's harmony of forest, sea, and mountain and all they represent, a theme no less eternally relevant for having been born out of those memories she claimed sprang from an earlier age. Hilda Ellis Davidson observes that a people's mythology is far more than a collection of amusing stories: 'It is the comment of the men of one particular age on the mysteries of human existence and the human mind, their model for social behavior, and their attempt to define . . . their perceptions of the inner realities'.[8] By viewing myth as man's attempt to express such ideas, Davidson claims and Sigrid Undset's work seems to illustrate, it is possible 'to discover more about our spiritual heritage, and perhaps to realise some of the defects in the spiritual development of the modern world. . . . In reaching out to explore the distant hills where the gods dwell and the deeps where the monsters are lurking, we are perhaps discovering the way home' (Davidson, *Gods and Myths*, pp. 21–2).

Since she was a child, Sigrid Undset had been familiar with the names by which the Old Norse had represented truths of human behaviour: Thor, the god of oaths and husbandmen; Freyr and Freyja, the deities of birth and harvest; Odin, the god of battle and of poetry. From her eleventh year she had been fascinated by Odin's pale warrior Skarphedin, but his secret had long eluded her. She had believed that he had brought on his family's ruin, but with the new insight that writing *Kristin Lavransdatter* had earned her, she grasped the essential mystery of his being, the hero's honour that is all that matters in a universe where evil is fated to overcome good. In the succession of betrayals of truth that shape human character, Sigrid Undset saw that disloyalty and the pain it causes are basic to the human condition, but just as surely as she worked her way through the personal and artistic challenges of her early years, she became aware that human fidelity to an ideal is so rare and so beautiful that it often can escape recognition entirely, as it had when she first read the *Njálá*.[9]

Devout Christian that he was, Lavrans Björgulfsson still stood for the ideals the Norse myths embodied in Thor, symbolised in the sacred pillars that upheld their homes and judgement seats. Like Thor who perished in Ragnarok, vanquishing the World Serpent who had fatally gnawed the roots of the tree Yggdrasil, Lavrans died having overcome his own sin, his loveless marriage, but he was himself bested by Kristin's betrayal, her sin against the Fourth Commandment. Kristin herself bears the characteristics of two Norse goddesses, the Vanir bride Freyja who oversaw human love, and the fertility deity Frigg, to whom Erlend quietly asked Ulf Haldorsson and old Aan to appeal when Kristin was in agonising labour for their first son. Both goddesses are represented in Old Norse art as weeping women, revealing the sorrow basic to woman's lot that Sigrid Undset had learned as lover, wife and mother.

Erlend Nikulausson, the most magnetic male figure in Sigrid Undset's work, lived in an age that no longer valued the ideals for which he existed. Erlend's ability to forgive, an attribute of his innate nobility, his physical courage, and his swift intuition all ensured the intrinsic superiority for which his fellows either loved or hated him. Like one of Odin's chosen, he possessed a kind of eternal youth, defying fate even on his deathbed with the warrior's dazzling grace; only the greatest of the old heroes could live and die alone in his own strength as Erlend did, refusing the Church's spiritual comfort because it came in the hands of the priest who had slandered Kristin.

Man's justice and woman's motherhood, Sigrid Undset maintains in *Kristin Lavransdatter*, in isolation can only perish, and for most human beings in this inimical universe mortal heroism demands too high a price to sustain the human spirit; there never have been many Erlend Nikulaussons. As she worked at Lillehammer in the early 1920s, living in the midst of Norway's stunning natural beauty and steeped in its sombre past, Sigrid Undset was recognising that the modern world she had explored so keenly in her earlier fiction rested on purely human values that were proving spiritually barren. To love truly, she had written earlier, a woman had to find a man she could call her lord. Kristin Lavransdatter had failed to acknowledge Erlend's spiritual gifts until it was too late for them on earth, but by living through Kristin's story, Sigrid Undset came to terms with her own life and accepted the most sacred myth of all, the heroism of Christ, who by his death bore witness to the greatest loyalty and offered humanity eternal salvation. Sigrid Undset was received into the Roman Catholic Church on 24 November 1924, the Feast of the Carmelite mystic St John of the Cross, and her marriage to Anders Svarstad was annulled.[10]

Notes

1. Charlotte Blindheim, *Moster Sigrid. Et familie portrett av Sigrid Undset*; translated in an excerpt published in *The Scandinavian Review*, vol. 70, no. 2 (June 1982), p. 52.
2. Harald Beyer, 'Sigrid Undset', in Einar Haugen (ed.), *A History of Norwegian Literature*, trans. Einar Haugen (New York: New York University Press, 1956), p. 5.
3. A.H. Winsnes, *Sigrid Undset: A Study in Christian Realism*, trans. P.G. Foote (New York: Sheed and Ward, 1953), p. 95.
4. Carl Bayerschmidt, *Sigrid Undset* (New York: Twayne, 1970), p. 38.
5. D.H. Lawrence, unpaginated Introduction to Frederick Carter's *Dragon of the Apocalypse*, in *Phoenix: The Posthumous Papers of D.H. Lawrence*, ed. Edward MacDonald (New York: The Viking Press, 1968 (1936)), p. 296.
6. Sigrid Undset, *The Mistress of Husaby*, trans. Charles Archer (New York: Knopf, 1921: repr. Bantam, 1978), p. 190.
7. Idem, *The Bridal Wreath*, trans. Charles Archer and J.S. Scott (New York: Knopf, 1920: repr. Bantam, 1978), p. 148.
8. Hilda R. Ellis Davidson, *Gods and Myths of Northern Europe* (New York and Harmondsworth: Penguin, 1964), p. 9.
9. Magnus Magnusson and Herman Palsson (trans.), Introduction, *Njal's Saga* (Harmondsworth and New York: Penguin, 1964), p. 13.
10. In *Les prix Nobel*, 1928, Sigrid Undset indicated that her marriage had broken up long before, a statement supported by her letter of 17 April 1922 to Nini Roll Anker, stating that at that time she was prepared to divorce Svarstad, but that she was holding off 'for the children's sake'. When she decided to join the Roman Catholic Church in 1924, she and Svarstad took steps to obtain a civil divorce, which Norwegian law specified had to be preceded by a year's separation, a circumstance which may have delayed her

formal conversion. As far as the Church was concerned, however, her 1912 marriage had been unlawful (because of Svarstad's divorce) and in 1924 all the Church required was her signature to a statement that the marriage was over and would not be resumed (Borghild Krane, *Sigrid Undset. Liv og meninger* (Oslo: Gyldendal, 1970), p. 65; my translation for this and all subsequent references).

6 Scandinavian Crime and Punishment: *The Master of Hestviken* 1925–1928

Thou dravest love from thee, who dravest Me.
Francis Thompson, 'The Hound of Heaven'

During some of the darkest days of the Second World War, Sigrid Undset found strength in recalling the mid-1920s, when her children were young and 'Mother', as she called herself in her reminiscence *Happy Times in Norway*,[1] had reached the peak of her creativity. Eleanor Roosevelt had asked her to write *Happy Times in Norway* for a youthful audience, and more than any other of her works, it reveals Sigrid Undset's maternal warmth, often overlooked because of the stern moral positions she advocated in her essays and the considerable intellectual and spiritual demands of her fiction.

Sigrid Undset's chief joys were the responsibilities of motherhood, and her family knew it. Charlotte Blindheim recalls twelve Christmases at Bjerkebaek that 'eclipsed each other in their gaiety. And in the middle is always Moster Sigrid . . . [her] figure stood as the perfect embrace and has remained so — always. She was a source of warmth for us during the holidays, but also every day — just in a different way'.[2]

Every parent learns that by explaining a truth to a child one often sees it in a powerful new light. For *Happy Times in Norway*, Sigrid Undset singled out three of her most special family memories from 1925: 'Merry Christmas'; 'The Seventeenth of May, Norway's Independence Day'; and 'Summer Vacation' at a *saeter* in the mountains where Kristin Lavransdatter might have walked. Each of these occasions revolved around the source of her maternal strength, an intense sense of duty born of love. She characteristically described it first in an image out of Norway's remote past, the Christmas sheaf of grain offered 'to the wild birds of our woods and mountains . . . the sacred gift of some thousands of years of Norwegian history to the powers of life and fertility, whatever name our ancestors gave to the Good Spiritual Forces watching over our home' (*Happy Times*, p. ix). The golden-haired grain goddess Sif was wife to Thor, and as Sigrid Undset told the story, he was 'the best god of all', because 'he heard the promise brides and bridegrooms and gave each other, and all the bargains and agreements men made'. Though Viking chieftains and their warriors worshipped Odin, the battle god imported from Saxon Germany, '[the] people at home, who struggled to win for themselves food from the earth and out of the sea, clung to Thor, the peasants' god and protector' (ibid., pp. 22–3). The sheaves of grain at Christmas symbolise the Norwegian farmers' deep loyalty to God, who created Nature for man's use, a loyalty that was integral to Sigrid Undset's being.

Nowhere could her devotion have been tested more severely than in her relationship with her only daughter. In 1925 her sons Anders and Hans were aged thirteen and seven; at ten, Tulla was epileptic, severely retarded and, according to Charlotte Blindheim, 'practically incapable of communicating with anyone except by touch' (*Scandinavian Review*, p. 49). Tulla was the heart of Sigrid Undset's household, and the bittersweet burden of her care was one of the pillars of Sigrid Undset's existence until the girl's death in 1939. 'When Mother came up from her workroom to rest, she would always take Tulla on her lap and sing to her' (*Happy Times*, p. 14), and though no one knew how Tulla knew, the child was always aware of 'happy times' to come in her own little world. Tulla had devoted nurses, including her stepsister Ebba Svarstad, but more than anyone else Sigrid Undset shouldered the costs and rewards of the responsibility Tulla represented. On the evening of Second New Year's Day, when everyone else had gone out to a party, 'God be praised, thought Mother, and drew Tulla still closer to her side — for it is an old belief in Norway that what one holds in one's hands when one sees the New Year's new moon, one shall not lose that year' (ibid., p. 61).

With her boys, Sigrid Undset, like every parent, had to grapple with the literal concept of truth children have. She once caught young Hans up on 'telling stories':

"But, Mother", he asked, "when you write books you make up what goes in them? Then you lie, don't you?" "At least the books I write are what we live on," said Mother curtly — but then she had to laugh. "People know that what is in books is not true in the sense that everything has happened just that way." (ibid., p. 79)

Sigrid Undset had come to see that truth and her duty were inseparable. In 1940, she looked back upon her conversion to Catholicism as an intellectual progress:

> By degrees my knowledge of history convinced me that the only thoroughly sane people, of our civilization at least, seemed to be those queer men and women which the Catholic Church calls the Saints . . . [who] seemed to know the true explanation of man's undying hunger for happiness — his tragically insufficient love of peace, justice, and goodwill to his fellowmen, his everlasting fall from grace.[3]

She admitted that when people seek the truth, they risk losing their comfortable illusions by finding it, but nevertheless: 'I had ventured too near the abode of truth in my researches about "God's friends," as the saints are called in the Old Norse texts. . . . So I had to submit' (*Twentieth Century Authors*, p. 1433).

Sigrid Undset had always told the truth as she saw it in her books, but after her conversion in late 1924 she became increasingly concerned with truth as the earthly evidence of man's loyalty to God, and during Easter Mass in 1925 at Monte Cassino, she suddenly glimpsed the connection of truth and duty in an intimate new way, with ideas she had heretofore grasped only intellectually becoming

> illuminated by an object-lesson . . . the communion of the saints . . . the untold souls who have lived through the ages, each of them imprisoned in the ravelled net of his own self, from which no doctrine can set us free, only God, and He only by dying on a cross . . . one can understand it, but sometimes it seems as if one can *see* it.[4]

Once Sigrid Undset had seen the 'reality of eternity and of the spirit' that she had merely understood before, that God's own sacrifice alone could break the net of man's self, she set about sharing it with the world in a novel, the vehicle that she had spent most of her adult life learning to use. Again her setting was fourteenth-century Norway; since 1905 she had been pondering her theme, humanity's fatal thirst for personal vengeance; and her hero, pale as Skarphedin, was Olav Audunsson, master of Hestviken, who had to hazard his soul before he could allow his Lord to save it.

Calling attention to the joy and anguish of parenthood that he represents, Sigrid Undset gave Kristin's father Lavrans Björgulfsson a small but pivotal appearance in *The Master of Hestviken*, slightly earlier than the action of *Kristin Lavransdatter*. In the last half of the thirteenth century, Norway had already begun to slip toward union with Sweden and Denmark, its ancient warrior aristocracy drained by conflict with the *Birkebeiner* a century earlier and fatally weakened by Magnus Law-mender's sweeping Christian reforms. By 1274, Magnus had repealed the old *wergild* laws and instituted a new legal code that accepted the concept of crime as an offence against the state rather than against an individual; he also enlisted the support of the Church, so that although his son Erik was a minor at Magnus' death in 1280, the aristocracy could not place its own king on Norway's throne. Through the nineteen years of Erik Priest-hater's reign and the twenty years his brother Haakon Magnusson ruled, the power, influence, and even the dignity of the *lendermaend* continued to decline, although for a time enough of their spirit remained to defend Norway against invaders. Erlend Nikulausson's cousin Munan Baardsson, an historical figure, had beaten Swedes led by Duke Erik away from King Haakon's new capital residence, the Akershus at Oslo, in a battle where Sigrid Undset's protagonist Olav Audunsson was grievously wounded.

Sigrid Undset made Olav's Hestviken an old chieftain's seat at the north end of the Oslofjord, well-used by Hestvik shipmen before St Olaf forbade Norwegians to go marauding in the eleventh century. All of the manor but its barn had been burned by the *Birkebeiner* two hundred years later in the time of Olav Audunsson's grandfather, when the *Birkebeiner* King Haakon the Lame defeated his rival, Erlend Nikulausson's ancestor King Skule, whom Olav Audunsson's family had supported. Olav Audunsson's times, like Kristin Lavransdatter's, have relatively little historical documentation, again allowing Sigrid Undset the artistic freedom to probe the human heart without worrying unduly whether 'everything happened just that way'.

The men of Hestviken, like many Norwegians, had long memories; and such men found that the renunciation of personal vengeance as an answer to mankind's eternal problem of evil and suffering was all the harder because of their powerful sense of honour. Olav Audunsson is one of the strongest, and Sigrid Undset traces his life through successive stages of reconciliation to the fatal disease that life itself presents, sealing each stage of his journey with a free choice that entails profound spiritual consequences. The first two volumes of *The Master of Hestviken*,[5] called in the English translation *The Axe* and the *The Snake Pit*, pursue Olav to the depths a human soul can reach, while the third and fourth, *In The Wilderness* and *The Son Avenger*, follow him to the height of Christian aspiration, God's loving salvation. At the nadir of Olav's fall, Lavrans Björgulfsson, a shining young knight's son himself as yet untainted by the world's pain, offers an act of loving kindness that eventually shows Olav the way to peace.

The Axe (1925)

Because Sigrid Undset made all the rest of Kristin Lavransdatter's life, for both good and ill, proceed from one momentary act, the promise she and Erlend Nikulausson exchanged in the first rapture of their love, Sigrid Undset's first great medieval novel embodies the truths of human behaviour lodged in the old myth of Thor, god of oaths, and his golden-haired wife Sif, goddess of fertility. With Olav Audunsson's story, Sigrid Undset turns to a darker human relationship, the clash between the loyalty of 'the people at home' to the communal values their protector Thor represents and the perilous surging Viking vitality born of the worship of Odin, the Saxon god of individual might in battle, poetry, and magic.

After briefly revealing Olav's lonely childhood as the victim of a hasty bargain struck between his dying father and Olav's foster-father Steinfinn Toresson, Sigrid Undset develops Olav's lifelong conflict, the 'net of self' he twists around his own throat when he chooses to wed Ingunn Steinfinnsdatter, not by honourable negotiation but by possessing her secretly long before her parents' death as a result of a vengeful raid to restore Steinfinn's honour. In the first section of *The Axe*, 'Olav Audunsson Takes a Wife', the initial betrayal of Steinfinn's trust bears bitter fruit; Olav lies to Arnvid, Ingunn's saintly cousin and his own closest friend, claiming he and Ingunn made a common law marriage with Steinfinn's blessing before he died.

Like Kristin's promise to Erlend, Olav's youthful and untruthful choice of Ingunn, virtually the only lyric moment in an otherwise sombre story, establishes the course of his entire life. In a quarrel at a monastery guesthouse in Hamar, Ingunn's cousin Einar insults Arnvid, who is pleading Olav's cause before Bishop Torfinn. Olav cuts Einar down with Kinfetch, his ancestral axe from Hestviken. In Olav's defence, an old lay brother claims that 'Einar spoke such words that in old days any man would have judged he died an outlaw's death by Olav's hand' (*Master of Hestviken*, p. 132). Even Einar's brother Haftor declares that the old laws which would have allowed him to slay his brother's killer were 'better suited to men of honour' than the new laws Haftor dismisses as 'dirty', because they were 'better for such fellows as Olav there, who outrage the daughters of our best houses and strike down their kinsmen when they call them to account' (ibid., p. 132). When Olav is imprisoned, his rage boils up 'with a sudden, voluptuous joy' like the battle lust Odin sent to his *berserker* warriors. This rage sustains Olaf through his escape from Norway and ten years of exile.

The second half of *The Axe*, 'Ingunn Steinfinnsdatter', is the only major segment of *The Master of Hestviken* not seen through Olav's eyes. Upon Einar's death, the Crown attaches Olav's Norwegian holdings, and Olav leaves Norway to become liegeman to Earl Alf Erlingsson, a mighty lord himself in exile, whom Olav loves and serves until 1289. After the departure of Olav, 'the only firmness in her weak, instinct-governed soul' (ibid., p. 166), Ingunnn lives in limbo, surrounded by indifferent relatives and spiteful servants. Neither maid nor wife, Ingunn rejects an honourable offer of marriage from one suitor only to fall into the arms of Teit, an itinerant clerk from Iceland, and when Olav returns grimly bent on taking Ingunn back to Hestviken as his bride, Ingunn has to reveal her pregnancy. Despite his revulsion, Olav's pride and her vulnerability deceive him into believing his soul will be healed it he protects her against the world. Later, at a lonely *saeter* on a winter night, fate puts Teit into Olav's hands;

even though Olav has left Kinfetch behind, the axe singing ominously as he set out, Teit's sword is no match for Olav's work-axe, and for shaming his Ingunn, who had not been altogether unwilling, Olav kills the boy he has reluctantly came to like. Olav leaves the body in the old way, sword on breast and food and water nearby as offerings, and sets the hut ablaze, judging himself and Ingunn avenged by the ancient code at least: 'A woman's honour — that was the honour of all the men who had the duty and right of watching over her' (ibid., p. 260).

When Ingunn's son Eirik is born and at her own wish is taken from her, Ingunn attempts suicide, but Arnvid saves her for Olav, whose one weakness, his powerlessness in the presence of helpless suffering, ensnares him. Like two children abandoned in a world that has lost its meaning, Olav and Ingunn reaffirm their vow in a kiss made sterile by one another's tears, rebels against the Christian law of forgiveness each has rejected so easily.

The Snake Pit (1925)

The second volume of *The Master of Hestviken* writhes in one unbroken skein of suffering that chronicles Olav Audunsson's twelve years of marriage. The title refers to the carvings on the ancient doorpost, saved from the ashes of the old manor, that now holds up the lintel of Hestviken's hall. As Olav enters his own house for the first time since he was seven, the figure of Gunnar from the *Volsungasaga* greets him, wreathed in serpents and bitten to the heart by the one snake he could not charm. Although Olav's careful husbandry makes Hestviken flourish once more and he takes his rightful place as the most influential landowner of the area, serpentine self-doubts pursue him. As handsome and irresistible to women as his great-uncle Torgils Foulbeard had been before his mind gave way under the weight of his sins, Olav fights down bodily temptation while Ingunn brings forth one dead or dying child after another; but the viper of pride continues to gnaw his breast, and Ingunn, far from being his helpmate, becomes the heaviest cross he has to bear.

After Ingunn at last produces a living son, Olav's pity and gratitude cause him to bring Eirik, the son she had abandoned for

Olav, to Hestviken. But little Audun Olavsson dies in his father's arms and Olav finds Eirik's propensity for lying impossible to bear, although the boy loved Olav 'better than anyone else on earth' (ibid., p. 426). Olav nevertheless offers to take the boy in hand as he would his own son, but Ingunn will not trust her husband with her lover's child. Olav finally unburdens his heart completely to his friend Arnvid Finnsson, though not to God: '"*You* have never known what it is to live at enmity with Christ"' (ibid., p. 441). Olav deceives himself into thinking he had then ceased rebelling against God, believing that he now loved God with all his mind and all his heart: '"I knew not that such love was within the power of man until I myself had abandoned His covenant and lost Him"' (ibid., p. 441), but by attempting to bargain with God with only outward piety and charity, Olav forgets the other half of Christ's commandment: to love his neighbour as himself. When he confesses to Arnvid that he murdered Teit, Arnvid promises to care for Ingunn if Olav will submit to ecclesiastical justice; but Olav cannot grant Ingunn and Eirik the same grace that he asked for himself, the trust in God to sustain them if Olav were to place himself in God's hands. Like a man foolishly trying to bargain against a fatal illness, Olav refuses to abandon his pride by throwing himself on the mercy of the Church, the only means to salvation Christianity knew in the Middle Ages. '"Think you", asked Arnvid, "that it avails you to offer God this and that — promise Him all that he has never asked of you — when you would withhold from Him the only thing you yourself know that He would beg of you?"' (ibid., p. 443).

Olav replied: '"The only thing? But that is *everything*, Arnvid — honour"' (ibid., p. 443). The personal honour to which Olav clings at last costs him Ingunn; the blooming health of one last child, Cecilia, drains the last vestiges of Ingunn's own, and she wastes away before Olav's eyes. That Lent, Arnvid dies as a monk, and knowing that no living man now shares his secret, Olav finally asks Ingunn to join him on a pilgrimage to Nidaros to confess not only the murder but their youthful sin that began it all. Olav, at twenty-eight, for the first time looks at his wife not as a pitiable child but as an adult with a Christian soul.

Olav can 'no longer bear to be God's enemy' and he offers to make his peace with God, but Ingunn once again fatally demands his pity and refuses to let him seek the help his own soul needs. When he is summoned to her deathbed from Hamar, Olav has to borrow a horse from a 'tall fair lad with silky, flaxen hair . . . one of the sons of the knight of Skog' (ibid., p. 499). Olav suddenly sees by comparison what he himself has become: 'a lesser man than Lavrans Björgulfsson in everything, stature and worship and power . . . he [Lavrans] looked as though destined to take his course through the world without ever meeting sorrow' (ibid., p. 505). At the end of his marriage and Ingunn's life, Olav stands alone, his fingers tracing Hestviken's ancient doorpost with 'snakes wreathed about the figure of Gunnar', and one viper devouring his own heart with the cold indifference more deadly to the soul than his earlier raging rebellion or smouldering pride. At the midpoint of Olav Audunsson' life, Sigrid Undset makes the master of Hestviken realise by comparing his lot to Lavrans' that a man must lose his life before he can find it.

In the Wilderness (1927)

Ironic as Lavrans Björgulfsson's brief appearance in Olav Audunsson's life seems in the light of the events of *Kristin Lavransdatter*, the sight of Lavrans' happiness underscores for Olav the enormity of his own sins, the pivotal point for the novel Sigrid Undset made of his life. The third volume, *In the Wilderness*, leads Olav on a different pilgrimage than he had once dreamed of making to Nidaros, for here he confronts the false god his selfish pride built for him.

In the first section, 'The Parting of the Ways', Ingunn has been gone for some years, Eirik and Cecilia are growing up, and Olav, now thirty-seven and well aware that he has rejected God's call to confess, takes ship for England on a trading trip. Walking with Olav Audunsson through thirteenth-century London is one of the masterstrokes of Sigrid Undset's fiction, a dazzling bombardment of sights, sounds, smells all throwing new doors open to Olav, while the Church Universal extends him a new insight into his spiritual predicament. As he listens to a martyr's Mass one morning in a new Dominican church in London, Olav 'felt the Spirit of God as a cleansing wind . . . that "breaks up the half-formed ice . . . before winter comes"' (ibid., pp. 550–1). Christ's

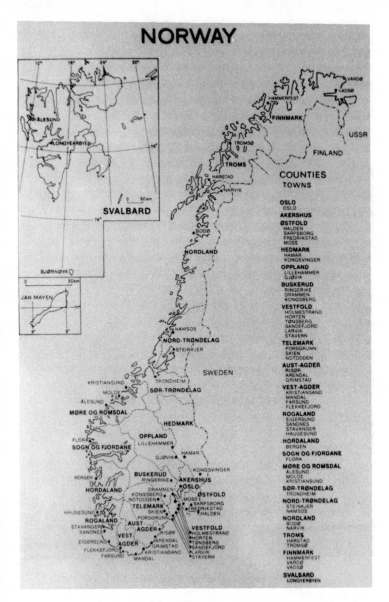

NORWAY

SVALBARD

NY ÅLESUND
LONGYEARBYEN

BJØRNØYA

JAN MAYEN

VARDØ
VADSØ
HAMMERFEST
FINNMARK
USSR
FINLAND
TROMSØ
TROMS
HARSTAD
NARVIK
BODØ
NORDLAND
NAMSOS
NORD-TRØNDELAG
STEINKJER
SWEDEN
KRISTIANSUND
MOLDE
ÅLESUND
TRONDHEIM
SØR-TRØNDELAG
MØRE OG ROMSDAL
HEDMARK
FLORA
OPPLAND
LILLEHAMMER
SOGN OG FJORDANE
GJØVIK
HAMAR
BERGEN
KONGSVINGER
BUSKERUD
RINGERIKE
AKERSHUS
HORDALAND
DRAMMEN
OSLO
KONGSBERG
ØSTFOLD
HAUGESUND
NOTODDEN
MOSS
TELEMARK
SARPSBORG
ROGALAND
SKIEN
FREDRIKSTAD
STAVANGER
PORSGRUNN
HALDEN
SANDNES
AUST
AGDER
VESTFOLD
RISØR
HOLMESTRAND
EIGERSUND
VEST
ARENDAL
HORTEN
AGDER
GRIMSTAD
TØNSBERG
FLEKKEFJORD
KRISTIANSAND
SANDEFJORD
FARSUND
MANDAL
LARVIK
STAVERN

COUNTIES
TOWNS

OSLO
OSLO

AKERSHUS

ØSTFOLD
HALDEN
SARPSBORG
FREDRIKSTAD
MOSS

HEDMARK
HAMAR
KONGSVINGER

OPPLAND
LILLEHAMMER
GJØVIK

BUSKERUD
RINGERIKE
DRAMMEN
KONGSBERG

VESTFOLD
HOLMESTRAND
HORTEN
TØNSBERG
SANDEFJORD
LARVIK
STAVERN

TELEMARK
PORSGRUNN
SKIEN
NOTODDEN

AUST-AGDER
RISØR
ARENDAL
GRIMSTAD

VEST-AGDER
KRISTIANSAND
MANDAL
FARSUND
FLEKKEFJORD

ROGALAND
EIGERSUND
SANDNES
STAVANGER
HAUGESUND

HORDALAND
BERGEN

SOGN OG FJORDANE
FLORA

MØRE OG ROMSDAL
ÅLESUND
MOLDE
KRISTIANSUND

SØR-TRØNDELAG
TRONDHEIM

NORD-TRØNDELAG
STEINKJER
NAMSOS

NORDLAND
BODØ
NARVIK

TROMS
HARSTAD
TROMSØ

FINNMARK
HAMMERFEST
VARDØ
VADSØ

SVALBARD
LONGYEARBYEN

Map of Norway

Altar, Nidaros Cathedral, Trondheim, Norway

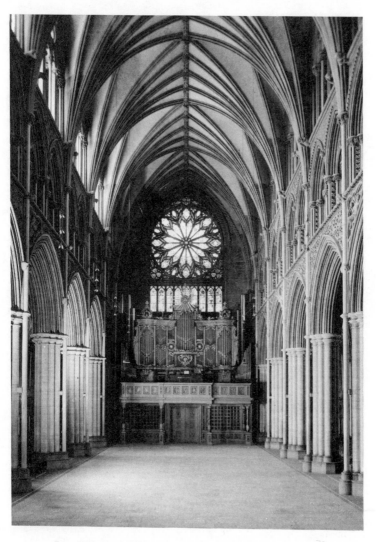
Rose Window, Nidaros Cathedral, Trondheim, Norway

Nidaros Cathedral (exterior), Trondheim, Norway

Karl-Johansgade, Oslo, Norway 1905 — Dissolution of Union with Sweden

Bjerkebaek: Sigrid Undset's home at Lillehammer, Norway

Sigrid Undset in Norwegian national dress

Sigrid Undset in her middle years

Sigrid Undset in old age

promise of 'not peace, but a sword' captivates Olav's warrior soul, hungry for individual salvation, and he feels a momentary call to the Knights Templar, that powerful crusading order of warrior monks, in 'the song of praise from a choir of men on guard against the approach of night' (ibid., p. 559).

Olav is also tempted by a young wife eerily like Ingunn, in an episode often criticised as an intrusive homily on Catholic doctrine. Gustafson believes: 'Seldom, if ever . . . has Sigrid Undset been so tasteless in her choice of narrative episode'.[6] Perhaps, however, she could find no way short of Olav's near-fall into adultery to allow him to recognise the nature of his sin as pride, the fatal *superbia* the medieval Western Church considered the deadliest of all man's rejections of God's grace. Like the Apostle Peter, Olav had to choose three times: Christ had first spoken to him from the Cross the night of Ingunn's death, when he met Lavrans; then 'He had spoken to him [Olav] in His holy church' (*Master of Hestviken*, p. 584); and 'now this last thing had befallen him, so that he was forced to see what manner of man he was and what was his sin' (ibid., p. 584).

When Olav Audunsson grasps the truth he had evaded so long, 'that his greatest sins were the sins of others no less than of himself' (ibid., p. 585), he suddenly feels he is as insignificant a sinner as the next man, and his pride collapses; Christ's promised sword 'sank into the most hidden roots of his being', and he feels himself 'sinking beneath the ice-cold waters of the very ocean' (ibid., p. 585). He sees, horribly, that his sins have choked all of his good deeds, and that he lied to Arnvid out of pride. Pride is notoriously hard to extinguish, however, and despite this step towards self-knowledge, Olav takes up his old responsibilities at Hestviken again, the life that he thinks can hide him from his God.

In the second part of *In the Wilderness* Olav discovers that all fire has disappeared from his life because 'He had chosen himself so long that he had lost his love of God', but acknowledging the cause of his indifference is his first step to a cure for his soul. Men he had known long ago began to reappear, and in a parallel to his own experience he agrees to foster Bothild, the daughter of a dying friend. Sixteen-year-old Eirik, whom Olav names as his heir, still lies compulsively, fearing that someone will come between him and the father he loves above all else. When Eirik insults Torhild, the robust woman who keeps Olav's house, loves him, and bears him a strapping son, Olav takes out his own frustrations on the boy, beating Eirik senseless. When he recovers, Eirik runs away to take service with one of King Haakon's knights at Oslo.

In 1308, when Olav is forty, Duke Erik of Sweden invades Norway, and Olav himself takes up arms, rousing the men of his district against the Swedes and their German mercenaries who are besieging the Akershus. His old axe Kinfetch sings again for Olav on the eve of battle, and once more Norwegian warriors chant Odin's ancient call to individual glory:

> Cattle die,
> kinsmen die,
> last dies the man himself;
> one thing I know
> that never dies;
> the fame of each man dead!
> (ibid, p. 709)

Olav's men drive off the invaders, but Olav lies wounded and disfigured, having chosen suffering that this time, he feels, has been of use: 'No pain could take from him the joy of having had the chance to stand up and fight for his home . . . sufferings that are of some *avail*, they are like the spear-points that raise the shield on which the young king's son sits when his subjects do him homage' (ibid., p. 715–16).

The Son Avenger

The section 'Winter', bleak and long as the endless frozen Northern night, opens *The Son Avenger*, the last volume of *The Master of Hestviken*. Olav's striking masculine beauty and grace have gone forever; he 'must think himself old' (ibid., p. 717); and a wound to his mouth garbles his speech, distancing him still more from his fellows as he settles into rebuilding Hestviken, ravaged by the Swedes on their way to Oslo. In another unpleasant reminder of his own youth, Olav takes in Aslak, a young man wanted for murder, with whom Cecilia falls in love, though Olav opposes her choice. Eirik feels a strong attraction to his foster-sister Bothild, but he mistakenly suspects his father would forbid him to marry her, and when Bothild suddenly dies of tuberculosis, Eirik as abruptly decides to serve God. Olav's heart begins to thaw as he watches Eirik, dressed as a bridegroom, take his novice's vows in the same Minorite church where Olav, waiting for Lavrans Björgulfsson to bring him a horse as Ingunn lay dying, had glimpsed Christ in the strangely living crucifix above the altar. Later, Olav gives his consent for Cecilia to marry Eirik's friend Jörund, even though Olav instinctively distrusts the man and his family. The farther he slips into middle age, the more Olav dreads the day when his children will leave him alone, a prisoner of his own sins.

One day the hand of God blends past and present for Olav Audunsson in a strange experience of *déjà vu*; he sees Ingunn stretching out her hands to him beside a brook — 'he could not tell whether it was to receive him or forbid him to come nearer' (ibid., p. 803). God's justice intervenes as Olav collapses from a stroke and falls at the water's edge. 'But at the bottom of his soul, deeper than doubt and disquietude, lay joy. He had seen that death had not yet parted him from her, and that his own youth was living somewhere in time and space, in spite of all he had done to kill it' (ibid., p. 804).

After ten years of living outside the law, twelve years of watching Ingunn die by inches, and thirteen years' loneliness after her death, Olav 'must follow the course that his heart had prompted all these years — fall at the feet of Christ crucified and confess that he had lived the whole time secretly at war with God and now knelt before Him, vanquished' (ibid., p. 807). Circumstances frustrate Olav's resolution to confess to Eirik, though, for the stepson Olav took so long to learn to love leaves the monastery, an apparent victim of his inability to tell the same story twice. A miserable chain of events caused by Jörund's deceit breaks off the match Olav then makes for Eirik with a suitable young woman, whose maligned older sister Eldrid Eirik then takes as his wife. By Olav's wish Eirik lives with Eldrid far from Hestviken, where Cecilia is struggling with the husband who abuses her.

When Jörund is found stabbed with the three-sided dagger Olav long ago gave Cecilia, Olav, stricken by guilt, begs her to join him in confession, drawing his life towards its climax. Enraged, Eirik narrowly misses killing Olav with Kinfetch, and Olav leaves Hestviken to make his peace with God, tormented by the belief that his daughter has become a murderess; 'hell has become his home'. Only the Bishop who lies dying this Saturday before Palm Sunday can give Olav absolution, but at last Olav breaks down all the bridges to his pride, confessing all before Father Finn Arvidsson and the least of his fellows in a lowly inn — everything but the identity of Teit, his victim so long ago. Banned now from the sacraments that could have healed him, Olav accepts his fate: '. . . here on earth it would never be his to see the radiance of a standard under which he might fight with the powers that were given him at his birth' (ibid., p. 959). When Eirik comes to tell him that a servant, not Cecilia, had killed Jörund, Olav collapses with a second stroke, half paralysed, 'like a tree that is blown down' (ibid., p. 961). The choice Olav finally makes in that spiritual winter grants him the grace of a voiceless living purgatory; but if such a winter came, Sigrid Undset implies God's spring, and the resurrection of Easter, could not be far behind.

The Son Avenger closes *The Master of Hestviken* on a note of redemption. Olav gives his consent for Cecilia to marry Aslak, and Eldrid and Eirik, who stayed at Hestviken to care for Olav, agree to seek the convent and the monastery after he dies. Close to the end, Olav glimpses Ingunn walking down a path a little ahead of him; he struggles to follow, and beside the Oslofjord at daybreak, knowing himself a thane who has disgraced his Lord, one 'who had not defended the standard and had stained the sword with dishonor and forgotten what the ring should have called to mind' (ibid., p. 986), Olav none the less receives a premonition of eternal bliss. As he lies dying, he 'heard sentence passed on his own life by the mouth of his son', who to Olav's eternal credit found 'a handful of good corn among the weeds of sin' (ibid., p. 992). Eirik himself leaves Hestviken to prosper in Cecilia's hands and rejoins the Minorite friars at Hamar. When after a gruelling journey to Nidaros he dies at sixty in his brothers' arms, Sigrid Undset names him Eirik Olavsson for the first and only time, acknowledging him as the son of Olav Audunsson, and the master of Hestviken.

Throughout Olav's long and painful life, he never abandons his faith in God, nor does he fail in any of the outward good works that the Church felt necessary to guide the Christian soul to heaven, but by denying himself confession and absolution, the earthly means to grace extended by the Church to man, Olav risks his immortal soul, illustrating the basic Roman Catholic doctrine Sigrid Undset had espoused: salvation cannot exist outside the Church.

While she was writing *The Master of Hestviken*, Sigrid Undset also took it upon herself to battle with the paganism she saw in modern times. A.H. Winsnes provides a detailed chronicle of her attempts to encourage modern civilisation to save itself in the battle between secular ideologies and 'those accepted by men who neither wish nor are able to free themselves from the Christian ideal . . . which claims that no society worthy of humanity can be established on earth, unless it finds its support in a power not of this world'.[7] Just after her conversion, she publicly disputed with Norwegian Lutheran authorities over the submission of their Church to the Norwegian state, and in three forceful articles, 'The Inheritance Which Must be Accepted', 'What Catholicism Thinks of Luther', and 'The Lutheran Spirit and the Catholic Spirit' as well as her short book *Catholic Propaganda* (1927), Sigrid Undset attempted to demonstrate that certain Lutheran policies paved the way for the totalitarian concept of the state, since Luther had not only broken with the Roman Catholic Church but had made his new Church submissive to individual German princes. Even Sigrid Undset's most sympathetic commentators observe that her position, though defended with intense and seemingly 'irrefutable' logic, lacks objectivity, because it reflects life in a country where Catholicism had long been outlawed and where in 1927 'there were stronger prejudices to overcome than at present [Winsnes was writing in the 1940s], if one was to undertake a cultural struggle on behalf of Catholicism' (Winsnes, *Sigrid Undset*, p. 161). Despite the rigour of her anti-Protestant polemics, which may indeed have been fortified by her lifelong distaste for things and persons German, Sigrid Undset's convictions demand respect even when they cannot be accepted wholesale. As time passes, her words have taken on new significance; it becomes easier, after two world wars, to value her ideas, especially her opinion that modern egocentricity, like Olav Audunsson's in the fourteenth century, which Barbara Tuchman aptly calls 'a distant mirror'[8] of our own times, is responsible for much of man's suffering and the evil it causes, from Auschwitz to the Gulag Archipelago — and beyond.

In 1928 Sigrid Undset received the Nobel Prize for Literature, inscribed 'principally with regard to her powerful pictures of Northern life in the medieval times'. Characteristically she donated the 15,000 Norwegian crowns to the Norwegian Authors' Association. The gold medal she kept for a little while; but later, like Olav Audunsson, she surrendered the best she had to a cause far outstripping individual pride.

Notes

1. Sigrid Undset, *Happy Times in Norway*, trans. Joran Birkeland (New York: Knopf, 1942).
2. Charlotte Blindheim, *Moster Sigrid. Et familie portrett av Sigrid Undset*; trans. in an excerpt published in *The Scandanavian Review*, vol. 70, no. 2 (June 1982), p. 52.
3. Stanley J. Kunitz and Howard Haycroft (eds.), *Twentieth Century Authors* (New York: H.W. Wilson, 1942; 7th printing, 1973), p. 1,433.
4. Quoted in Carl Bayerschmidt, *Sigrid Undset* (New York: Twayne, 1970), p. 41.
5. See 'Bibliographical Notes', p. 150. Quotations below are from the New American Library Plume edition.
6. Alrik Gustafson, 'Christian Ethics in a Pagan World', in *Six Scandinavian Novelists* (Minneapolis, Minn.: University of Minnesota Press, 1968), p. 349.
7. Quoted in A.H. Wisnes, *Sigrid Undset: A Study in Christian Realism*, trans. P.G. Foote (New York: Sheed and Ward, 1953), p. 158.
8. Barbara W. Tuchman, *A Distant Mirror* (New York: Alfred A. Knopf, 1978).

7 Catholic Propaganda: 1928–1940

> The world is charged with the grandeur of God
> . . .
> Why do men then now not reck his rod?
> Gerard Manley Hopkins, 'God's Grandeur'

Martin Seymour-Smith claims that when reporters approached Sigrid Undset just after she won the 1928 Nobel Prize for Literature, she told them: 'I have not time to receive you. I am studying scholastic philosophy'.[1] Apocryphal or not, the remark reflects both Sigrid Undset's attitude toward the materialistic wasteland she felt Europe had become since 1914 and her conviction that its salvation lay solely through the official doctrine of the Roman Catholic Church.

Although Norway had remained neutral during the First World War, Sigrid Undset had seen the enormous human costs of the 'war to end all wars': 10 million dead and 20 million wounded, countless others 'shell-shocked', the women and children bereft at home — a whole generation devastated. Worse, the seeds of future conflict already were growing; Germany, whom popular opinion credited with starting the war, had not been represented at Versailles. Germany did not forgive.

Paradoxically, wartime technology soon raised Europe's post-war standard of living with medical breakthroughs, agricultural mechanisation and modernised industrial capacity. While Sigrid Undset was writing her great medieval novels in the 1920s, Europe was enjoying a welcome though illusory optimism in which even Germany shared, once the 1924 Dawes Plan had alleviated the breakneck inflation the German government had encouraged to avoid paying its war reparations.

The year 1905, when Norway broke with Sweden, had also ushered in two far-reaching events that contributed strongly to the anti-religious atmosphere of the 1920s. Freud's *Three Essays on the Theory of Sexuality*, 1905, had laid the foundation for psychological theories easily misinterpreted by the uninitiated to demonstrate erroneously that the individual was not responsible for his actions; that the human personality resulted from hereditary and childhood influences; and that sex was the primary motivation of human existence. Einstein's *Theory of Relativity*, also appeared in 1905, and virtually no one understood it; it was similarly misread to become the basis of the philosophical opinion that no absolute standard existed to measure human values. By the 1920s pragmatism dominated much popular thought, while art had taken two divergent paths, one into naturalism's grindingly objective portrayals of individuals trapped in an inimical universe, and the other into esoteric art for art's sake, constricting artists and audience to an ever-diminishing elite.

Since 1917, the Communist Party of the Soviet Union had been forcing a gigantic but backward nation into becoming a modern industrial state. Stalin used two famous provisions of Article 12 of the Soviet Constitution, 'He who does not work, neither shall he eat', and 'From each according to his ability, to each according to his needs', to rise to absolute dictatorship by 1928. European Communist Parties supported by the Soviet Union were particularly visible in Italy, Germany, and France, and though they exerted little political power in the 1920s, their mere existence sparked reactions which later gave impetus to the Nazi and Fascist movements.

Already by 1922, Communist attempts to seize power in Italy had fuelled sufficient unrest for Mussolini to become premier by force, and though Hitler's Beer Hall Putsch of 1925 was put down by the German Army, the principles he had outlined in *Mein Kampf*, 1924, won him by 1929 a power base of influential industrialists, a significant segment of the German press and a private militia. Fascism's glorification of the 'total state' in which the individual is submerged and the Fascist theory of Social Darwinism in which the strongest nations survive by crushing their more peaceful and complacent neighbours appealed most strongly to middle-class conservatives terrified by the possibility of political domination by the lower classes, a domination that socialism and even democratic egalitarianism seemed to be encouraging. Fascism offered salvation from 'mob rule' through the all-powerful leader, who purported to embody his nation's highest ideals. By 1930, Hitler was offering a seductive mixture of anti-Semitism and pseudo-Germanic mythology to a Germany chafing under postwar problems and eager for restitution, if not revenge; the Saxon god Wotan, whose deceptive runes and *berserker* rage Norwegian farmers had long distrusted, was about to take on a savage new incarnation.

Traditional Christianity also had its champions. A few thinkers in the mid- to late-nineteenth-century England, such as John Ruskin and Matthew Arnold, had already denounced materialism and agnosticism, and by 1900, two conservative French novelists, Paul Bourget and Maurice Barrés, demanded a return to patriotic and Roman Catholic values, influencing a younger generation of writers who formed the small Catholic Renewal Movement around 1914. G.K. Chesterton and Evelyn Waugh in England and François Mauriac and Paul Claudel in France, writers whom Winsnes says 'rediscover the eternal',[2] voiced the Roman Catholic position, calling for a return to tradition and faith as did other prominent writers, including T.S Eliot with Anglo-Catholicism; Aldous Huxley with Oriental mysticism; William Styron with traditional Protestantism and Bernard Malamud with Judaism.

In 1945, leading Norwegian intellectuals claimed that between the world wars Norwegian thought tended to lack '"firm guiding values, any conscious realisation of human worth and a sustaining ideal of life"' (quoted in Winsnes, *Sigrid Undset*, p. 155), but a few, of whom Sigrid Undset was distinguished because of her clearcut religious ideal, consciously advanced the Christian point of view. The religious position she had achieved by 1928 had taken a long time to evolve: *The Longest Years* shows that she possessed a strong moral idealism at an early age, and as she matured she adopted an ethical but non-institutional Christianity; but it took her intimate knowledge of the Middle Ages, the Age of Faith, to allow her to accept Roman Catholicism as 'the only religious institution which successfully avoids all of the pitfalls of mere sectarianism — a sectarianism originating in man's will to create a God in his own image'.[3]

Roman Catholicism holds many theological mansions. In the 1920s Sigrid Undset seemed most at home in Augustinian Christianity, taught to Olav Audunsson by Eirik's Minorite (Franciscan) vocation and to Kristin Lavransdatter by gentle Brother Edvin: '"There is no man nor woman, Kristin, who does not love and fear God, but 'tis because our hearts are divided twixt love of God and fear of the devil and fondness for the world and the flesh, that we are unhappy in life and death"'.[4] Both Kristin and Eirik at last cast the world away in the loving hope of a mystical union with God, the goal of St Francis' teaching.

After she completed *The Master of Hestviken*, Sigrid Undset's religious orientation reached its final phase, shifting from faith-centred Franciscan mysticism to scholasticism, which St Thomas Aquinas shaped into the official doctrine of the Roman Catholic Church. He reconciled faith and reason, insisting that reason has its own autonomy and defending reason against those who would suppress Aristotle as the father of heresy. Thomism views the universe as a series of creations ordered and crowned by God, Who is pure act. Human beings come to know of God's existence through the knowledge provided by their senses as a means of grasping universal principles. Since the opposite of being does not exist in the Thomistic universe, and since good and being are identical, scholasticism accepts the absence of good as evil, permitting the relation of scholastic principles to every aspect of human life and viewing sin and sorrow as parts of the Divine Plan.

In the 1920s, prominent French Catholic thinkers like Jacques Maritain led a resurgence of scholasticism called neothomism, applying Thomistic principles to modern economic, political, and social conditions. Norway had experienced a general cultural swing toward France after the First World War, and Sigrid Undset was strongly influenced by French Dominican priests, Aquinas' spiritual sons, especially Father A.J. Lutz, who had begun missionary work in Norway. Maritain and other neo-thomists urged Christians not merely to defend their ideals against the godless materialism of the times, but to attack it (ibid., p. 157); and few writers answered the call to battle as wholeheartedly as Sigrid Undset did. Her next two novels announced the thesis that she supported for the rest of her life: that the Church's dogmatic authoritarianism must replace postwar materialism if society was to survive. So much of her own spiritual journey to Roman Catholicism also appears in these novels that they represent some of her most important autobiographical statements; Sigrid Undset seems to have contemplated a 'novel of conversion' as early as 1919, and the issues of *Aftenposten* for 7 and 19 February 1920 contain an article that is word for word the first chapter of *The Wild Orchid*.[5]

The Wild Orchid (1929)

Master gardener that she was, Sigrid Undset chose to graft symbolic titles onto the neothomistic roots which anchor *The Wild Orchid*[6] and its sequel *The Burning Bush*. Her hero Paul Selmer has grown up in the confines of his mother's will; liberal, divorced, and self-sufficient, Julie Selmer had 'carried off her sons to fresh air and light and sunshine . . . to have a kind of respect for frail and tender things' (*The Wild Orchid*, p. 18). Although obeying Julie's pragmatic insistence that her sons maintain a relationship with their father and his new wife, Paul resents them both until the last summer of his boyhood, when he eagerly waits for Julie's transplanted wood orchids to bloom. Their mere existence in Norway was a wonder in itself, yet Paul was 'frightfully disappointed' in their fragile little blooms. As anticipation died in the face of reality, another of those devastations of maturity Sigrid Undset depicts so often and so well, Paul begins to see how he has misjudged the father he does not know, the man to whom he now realises his mother 'had quite coolly offered stones in place of bread' (ibid., p. 74). At the same time, he visits St Olav's Church in Oslo with his Catholic landlady, and his eyes open: 'for the first time . . . he could perceive some sense in divine service . . . that a Being was present to receive their souls' (ibid., p. 89).

Paul's attraction to Catholicism deepens steadily. On 7 June 1905, Norway's first Independence Day, he muses, '. . . yes, God — today he ought to have existed. . . . There ought to have been someone to whom one could give thanks and honour' (ibid., p. 99), an expression of man's archetypal need for a deity to worship. Paul also instinctively defends the Church's basic doctrine of both faith and good works as necessary for salvation against his horrified Lutheran relatives: ' "Good God — has it come to this, a Catholic in our family!" ' (ibid., p. 101).

A little later, Paul falls in love with Lucy Arneson, a young shop girl, in one of Sigrid Undset's most lyrical passages. They become lovers, and Paul consults his friend Harold Tangen, now a priest, about marriage. Although Paul had not yet become a Catholic, he receives 'a sudden knowledge of what a sacrament was' while he prays one night in St Olav's Church: 'If it was true that He was *here* [italics in original] . . . then He must also be present in another way everywhere and at all times . . . then the whole of life was inconceivably more serious and valuable than he had ever dreamt. . . . It is simply too good to be true' (ibid., pp. 226–7).

One of the lessons Sigrid Undset most strongly stresses in her later fiction is that outside the Church, purely human relationships are brief and 'too good to be true'. Paul's mystical insight, half-inspired by physical passion for Lucy, did not satisfy either his intellect or Sigrid Undset's. She and Paul both had to know as well as feel the God who called to them from the Catholic altar, and without knowledge of Him, the love Paul and Lucy shared was doomed. Paul fails to realise that his concern for Lucy, like Olav Audunsson's half-devoted, half-guilty loyalty to Ingunn, robbed her of human dignity as a being made in her Creator's image and endowed with free choice.

When Lucy abruptly leaves him and marries another man, Paul gropes after spiritual crumbs. Like many of his countrymen, Paul could easily understand swift martyrdom, 'how men have always had the courage to die', but ' "[it] is *living* without religion they don't manage so well" ' (ibid., p. 101). Paul's tender first love collapses because it lacks firm spiritual roots, and by August 1914, the worldly marriage he then slid unthinkingly into with Björg was on the brink of shattering, while all Europe tottered towards calamity.

The Burning Bush (1930)

A considerable leap of faith lies between *The. Wild Orchid* and *The Burning Bush*,[7] named for the willing sacrifice God exacts in return for eternal life. One Easter several years after his marriage, Paul Selmer joins the Roman Catholic Church, and once the war is over, he tries to put his neothomist principles into practice in his stonecutting business at Haugen, with mixed results; despite Paul's lofty theories, 'production increased at the expense of the work' (*The Burning Bush*, pp. 252–3). His marriage was in trouble, too: 'He had neglected her [Björg] always and tried to bribe her and himself with his everlasting compliance' (ibid., p. 257).

Paul makes the same mistake with Björg that he had made with Lucy; he had met neither woman 'as an equal, with a different kind of egotism from his own' (ibid., p. 141). Björg had come from a well-to-do family, but she was emotionally retarded, bored, unhappy, frustrated and lonely. Björg leaves Paul and their children only to return disgraced after being rejected by her lover, and she becomes a heavy burden for Paul to bear.

Paul Selmer's jealous God demands an even greater sacrifice. Lucy reappears, fleeing from her brutal husband Lövstö, and tells Paul that she broke their engagement because she had felt unworthy of him. Grievously tempted to yield to his newly profound love for her, Paul nevertheless resists an act his society would condone but his Church forbids. Shortly afterwards, Lövstö beats Lucy savagely, and Paul, defending her, is accused of Lövstö's death.

Awaiting trial for murder, Paul confronts the ultimate human holocaust, the sacrifice of his own self: '. . . he would never again feel his own ego as anything real . . . the only thing which really had existence, in himself and in everything, was God' (ibid., p. 450). In that Presence, both the verdict that Lövstö had died of natural causes and Lucy's death a few days later are merely postscripts to Paul's vision that Easter morning, at an improvised jailhouse altar, 'a symbol of God's will to accept all that is most bitter as His share' (ibid., p. 451). By offering up his life, Paul comes 'nearer the naked heart of the mysteries than he had ever been before' (ibid., p. 451), and the flame would warm him for the rest of his life.

Paul Selmer shares Erlend Nikulausson's physical courage and passion and Olav Audunsson's stubborn devotion to God; but Paul, like the apostle whose name he bears, makes his decision early enough in his life so that he can 'live according to [his] faith and *do* something for God's sake' (*The Wild Orchid*, p. 101). Like Sigrid Undset herself, Paul was 'a Catholic because he believed that the Church . . . begins by giving sober information about absolute truth' (*The Burning Bush*, p. 265). Once she had granted that Thomistic premise, Sigrid Undset served faithfully as a militant Christian, battling twentieth-century materialism and the new barbarism Hitler would soon unleash upon the world.

Quantitatively the 1930s were Sigrid Undset's most productive decade. Besides her 'novels of conversion', *The Wild Orchid* and *The Burning Bush*, she fictionalised her childhood in *The Longest*

Years, written in 1934, and she also developed the theme of salvation through Roman Catholicism in legendary, contemplative and historical modes. Her hagiographical narrative, *Hellig Olav, Norges konge* ('St Olaf, Norway's King') and the German meditation 'Das Weihnachtswunder' ('The Christmas Miracle') appeared in 1930. Disturbed by the ominous phenomenon of Adolf Hitler, she explored the relation between Christianity and German culture in *Begegnungen und Trennungen* ('Meetings and Partings'), discussed below. As if sensing that Christians would soon have to defend themselves unto death, she concentrated on the mystery of martyrdom in *Stages on the Road*, a collection of essays written between 1928 and 1932 and published in 1933; while the Reichstag was putting full dictatorial powers into Adolf Hitler's eager hands, the Catholic Church was investigating new candidates for sainthood.

Stages on the Road

In these resting places on her road of life, Alrik Gustafson believes that 'Sigrid Undset seems to have managed to shake off, at least for the moment, the narrower aspects of a purely Catholic dogma in the interests of a more inclusive, universal Christian view' (Gustafson, 'Christian Ethics', p. 357). These six essays also parallel the shift in the religious orientation of her fiction from the 1920s to the 1930s. 'Margaret Clitheroe' (1928) and 'Robert Southwell, S.J.' (1929) reflect the Augustinian–Franciscan position that what one must endure in this valley of tears matters only as a preparation for eternal life. Margaret Clitheroe and Robert Southwell lived and died under England's 1585 Act of Parliament which declared devotion to Catholicism an act of treason, a time when 'a man might be hanged for having stood a priest a tankard of ale'.[8] Margaret Clitheroe was pressed to death for harbouring fugitive priests. Southwell, author of the intense mystical poem 'The Burning Babe', escaped the prescribed disembowelment and quartering only by the intercession of the crowd who watched his hanging. As a Catholic in a country that for centuries had outlawed her faith, Sigrid Undset felt that 'those who had died to spread Christianity among mankind, had been martyrs for the Christianity of Rome and not for that of Geneva or Wittenburg' (*Stages on the Road*, p. 143).

By 1930, however, when she wrote 'Letter to a Parish Priest', Sigrid Undset focused less on extraordinary demonstrations of faith and more on the everyday trials of Christian life in an essentially pagan society. She had already accepted the family as a universal building block of society predating even Christianity (ibid., p. 255), and she believed that European morality and artistic values were so inextricably bound up with Christianity that rejecting them would mean cultural suicide.

Sigrid Undset also argued Thomistically that Christian marriage required formidable heroism, a quality dear to her Nordic heart: '. . . very few people would be able to endure each other if they were not bound together to serve some ideal which is so great as to make them both seem insignificant when measured against it' (ibid., p. 257). In the remaining essays of *Stages on the Road*, she examined 'lifelong monogamy', impossible to advocate, she said, 'unless one believes that every single human soul is worth God's dying to save it' (ibid., p. 257). She exemplified her marital ideal in Ramon Lull, a thirteenth-century Franciscan, and Angela Merici, 'a champion of the women's movement' who in the sixteenth century founded the Ursuline Order, nuns who worked outside the convent as 'officers in the Church Militant'. With Lull and Angela Merici, Sigrid Undset implies that the life given up gladly but quickly for God may be less demanding than the day-to-day struggle to live obedient to His given Laws, the theme of her novels after *Stages on the Road*, all examinations of the sacrifices in Christian marriage.

Several critics have observed that none of Sigrid Undset's characters finds happiness in an illicit love. Once Kristin's passion for Erlend had been consummated, their wills began to clash in a conflict that finally cost him his life. Olav Audunsson paid all his days for those guilty summer nights with Ingunn, and Paul Selmer had to shoulder the cross of a loveless marriage as his price for salvation. In 'Letter to a Parish Priest', Sigrid Undset insisted: 'If the delinquencies of one party are of such a nature as to render cohabitation impossible, the other must nevertheless feel himself bound to such an extent that he or she works for the welfare of both their souls, by prayer and penance and good deeds'.[9] Perhaps she lived that difficult credo herself; certainly she incorporated it into *Ida Elisabeth*, written in 1932, and *The*

Faithful Wife, experimental Christian novels in which she placed her heroines in naturalistic situations and sustained them with that stubborn loyalty peculiar to Scandinavia. A.H. Winsnes observes that such loyalty allowed these women to 'extract gold from the dross of everyday life, a glimpse of the eternally feminine, the prototype of womankind, in the Christian sense' (Winsnes, *Sigrid Undset,* p. 195).

Ida Elisabeth (1932)

Like Kristin Lavransdatter, Ida Elisabeth breaks her father's heart by an adolescent affair with a man he thinks unworthy of her; she marries her lover Fridjof Braatö more to justify herself than to create a Christian union. Fridjof, though superficially charming, proves to be worthless: losing jobs, squandering money, taking a mistress and even through his negligence contributing to the death of their oldest child, Sölve. After their divorce, Ida Elisabeth considers attempting a new life with Tryggve, her dependable and caring lawyer, but her children's claims override those of her heart, and she gives Tryggve up. After watching Fridjof die of tuberculosis, Ida Elisabeth receives one of those religious insights with which Sigrid Undset often rounded off her characters' lives: '. . . she recalled Fridjof's dead face as a sort of token that perhaps the incomprehensible would not always remain incomprehensible'.[10]

The Faithful Wife (1933)

More contemporary and more conventional than *Ida Elisabeth,* *The Faithful Wife* examines the break-up and reconstruction of marriage between Sigurd and Nathalie, two products of liberal thought. In the heady atmosphere of the mid-1930s, Communists, Nazis and Fascists all urged radical social views denying the traditional religious concept of marriage as a sacrament, and 'liberated' circles in Norway, as elsewhere, considered sexual experimentation near-obligatory. Even though Natalie has grown up in a free-thinking home and she believes she and her husband should freely pursue other interests, his actual infidelity devastates her. Sigurd's lover Adinda, a Catholic, refuses to consider giving up their child, forcing Sigurd to develop his own moral sensibility, and after Adinda dies in childbirth, Sigurd and Nathalie are reconciled, an anomalous ending in Sigrid Undset's fiction. Carl Bayerschmidt believes this novel fails to satisfy because the lack of a common goal that bedevils the marriage from the start is never made up; in Sigrid Undset's work, he observes, 'no other woman who fails to see the life of the senses as part of the divine plan finds happiness in marriage' (Bayerschmidt, *Sigrid Undset*, p. 147).

Like Ida Elisabeth, however, Nathalie does take a vital first step towards transcending the physical and reaching spiritual fulfilment as a wife and mother. Both heroines hold fast to promises they made while intoxicated with youthful sexuality; as Ida Elisabeth's father had been in the habit of saying, '. . . what one has signed in one's cups one must abide by when sober' (*Ida Elisabeth*, p. 132). The old Scandinavian proclivity for carrying out one's word is one of Sigrid Undset's stepping stones to the God of eternal life, and she condemns to disaster those who violate their obligations.

Sigrid Undset had already equated the contemporary rebellion against religious tradition with the dangerous decline in European national purposes, sensing the potential for catastrophe: '. . . when a people forgets its heroes or tries to deprecate them . . . it condemns itself to insignificance and cowardice and loses the instinct to defend itself against all that is inimical and alien to its nature' (*The Burning Bush*, p. 71).

Saga of Saints (1934)

In *Saga of Saints* Sigrid Undset reminded Norwegians of their spiritual heroes, tracing Norway's ancient history from its prehistoric settlements to the early fourteenth century, when Olav Audunsson and Lavrans Björgulfsson were young. She drew heavily on the *Heimskringla* ('Circle of the Earth') of Snorri Sturluson, the thirteenth-century skald and author of the *Prose Edda*, but whereas Snorri chronicled Norway's kings and chieftains from Olaf Tryggvasson to Sigurd Jorsalfar, Sigrid Undset focused on Norway's six great medieval saints, heroes of both spiritual and earthly battles: St Sunniva, an enigmatic woman martyr; St Olaf, 'Norway's King to All Eternity'; St Hallvard, akin to St Francis in holy humility; St Magnus, the martyred earl whose remains had been discovered in an Orkney cathedral in 1926; St Eystein, Archbishop of Nidaros, and St Thorfinn, the Bishop of Hamar who played an important role in Olav Audunsson's search for God. As a coda to her saga, Sigrid Undset added the story of Father Karl Schelling, a nineteenth-century Barnabite missionary who gave his life to Catholicism's 'second spring' in Norway.

Sigrid Undset believed that one of the constants of human behaviour was the paradoxical combination of man's longing for freedom with his craving for a leader. She felt that nineteenth-century Europeans had all too uncritically admired the ancient Vikings, failing to observe that while the 'wolves of the sea' maintained moral standards at home to avoid their fellows' revenge, what they did abroad was an entirely different matter, and she feared a re-enactment of Viking-style terrorism in the maelstrom that was devouring Europe in the mid-1930s.

Sigrid Undset also believed Norwegians had been able to outgrow their Viking culture and adopt Christianity because of the inherent similarity in the Viking and the early Christian outlooks: 'To the proudest among the Vikings defeat was no disgrace if a man's fame survived him. For the Christian, death was a gain if he died for a cause he considered immortal'.[11] Against the pessimism of the old belief that in a universe where even the gods must die, personal courage was all that counted, Christianity pitted the optimism that, as Sigrid Undset knew so well, 'does not come easily to one who has delved deeply into human nature, unless he can put his trust in something which is beyond the life he knows' (*Saga of Saints*, pp. 33–4). St Olav replaced Thor in Norway through the landed *bönder* who trusted in the sanctity of their oaths, rather than through the haughty Trönder lords who clung tenaciously to their pagan ways, pursuing 'the only things a man *can* win, honor and fame' (ibid., p. 150). As she studied Norwegian history, Sigrid Undset had learned that men do not always choose the best leaders when they rely on human understanding alone. Norway fell into its bondage, she said, by forgetting the vital question its hero-saints had asked: 'Lord, what can I do for Thee?' She also knew that man's yearning for a lord could be subverted: '. . . the people of Europe [today] are in revolt . . . casting away the good with the bad. They [are] driven onwards by a blind and instinctive hope that they may find leaders who solve the difficulties of reality because they have something of the mystic in them' (ibid., pp. 240–1). Those lessons from Norway's past helped Sigrid Undset formulate her next collection of essays, *Men, Women, and Places*, published in 1938, where she reflected on her faith in relation to literature and history, the areas of her own greatest professional achievements.

Men, Women and Places (1938)

One of the more exotic attempts Europeans of the 1930s made to 'solve the difficulties of reality' was spiritualism, a subject Sigrid Undset treated both in *The Burning Bush* and in her essay 'Blasphemy', published in 1935. Sigrid Undset took spiritualism every bit as seriously as Thomas Mann did in *The Magic Mountain*; she observed that most people have had 'occult' experiences in the sense of mysterious or inexplicable events, but she refused to class these as supernatural, still less as religious, which she defined as relating human beings to the divine. The practicality of her religious orientation appears clearly in another essay published that year, 'Cavalier', where she stressed not the physical but the economic martyrdom of English Catholics under stringent civil restrictions that lasted until 1926. In retelling the story of William Blundell, an English Catholic nobleman who died in 1698, she illustrated her key to Christian living: the world might well be a vale of tears, but 'it *is* God's work'.[12]

In 'The Strongest Power', 1936, Sigrid Undset again used England's religious Civil War as her springboard for declaring that 'love being stronger than hate and . . . good triumphing over evil . . . is sheer nonsense — when it is a question of natural love and purely human goodness' (*Men, Women and Places*, p. 163). In her consistently neothomistic interpretation of history, whether the absence of good men call evil is implemented by a Cromwell or by a Hitler, the hatred such tyrants engender is a 'far more uniform and rallying emotion' (ibid., p. 163) than the earthly love that constricts one's liberty. She believed man had only one defence against such evil, which usually assailed humanity in 'the disinclinations of the flesh, its indolence and sluggishness. . . . Unless our natural goodness and our natural, unstable love of truth are penetrated by *that* love and *that* truth which are synonyms of the Creator's power, we shall nevertheless fall victims to one or the other of the seven deadly sins' (ibid., pp. 165–6).

From the very beginning of her work, Sigrid Undset's most successful characters were those who persisted in faith and good works, stubbornly subduing those deceptively small but devilishly easy urges which lead to the abyss. Self-sacrificing motherhood had also been her touchstone for 'good works' from her earliest writing to her 1937 review essay on the contemporary Danish author Marie Bregendahl and her 1938 meditation on the well-travelled medieval mystic Margery Kempe, the occasion for Sigrid Undset's contention that medieval women were the world's first true feminists.

Increasingly, too, she was concerned with the international conflict she felt approaching. In her essay 'The Strongest Power' (1938), she commented that one must fight on two fronts to defend what was established, 'to change that which he would preserve' (ibid., p. 162). She had already remarked in her 1934 essay on Leo Weismantel, a contemporary German writer who shared her belief that pagan religions furnished a rich subsoil for Christianity, that Christianity now needed reinvigoration from its deepest roots, since Weismantel's work proved to her that even in 1934 Germany was beginning to pervert its genuine religious impulse into a pseudo-Teutonic racism.

Sigrid Undset's reverence for 'the spirit of place' also appears in the essays 'Summer in Gotland' and 'Glastonbury', records of her travels in the last years before the Second World War. She had always had an unusual sensitivity towards the places men instinctively held as holy, knowing that 'gods could be worshipped the better where the human heart could respond to the comely proportions of the landscape',[13] a view which led her to an outstandingly perceptive essay on D.H. Lawrence written between 1935 and 1938.

At first glance, Lawrence, who died in 1930, seems of all the writers of her generation the most antithetic to everything that Sigrid Undset stood for. Some critics hailed and most reviled his forthright presentation of a new concept of sexuality that he felt would enable men and women to be reborn to a new life of individuality, free of the egoistic demands that were leading their civilisation to disaster. Sigrid Undset could not accept his sexual prophecy, which she considered a result of the harmful puritanism of his youth, but she was nearly alone at that time in declaring Lawrence 'a visionary and a poet of genius' (*Men, Women and Places*, p. 41) who correctly saw that what he called 'a new relation'[14] must be established between man and God. Behind what she called Lawrence's 'incredibly hallucinatory art' Sigrid Undset glimpsed more accurately than any other contemporary critic 'the man of mystery who symbolizes his civilization at a moment of crisis. . . . Much of what is happening in Europe today is the brutal reaction of mass humanity to problems the genius D.H. Lawrence perceived and faced and fought against in his own way' (ibid., p. 53).

As Sigrid Undset was writing these essays, Hitler purged his Nazi Party and set up the first concentration camps in 1934; Italy conquered Ethiopia in 1935, and Stalin liquidated millions of his countrymen between 1936 and 1938, the year France and England yielded up Czechoslovakia to Nazi demands for *Lebensraum*. The old order of Europe was dying, and with it Sigrid Undset's career as a novelist.

Madame Dorthea (1939)

In 1939, Sigrid Undset lost both her daughter Tulla and her mother, who had recently joined the Catholic Church, the only one of her family besides Hans, a baptised Catholic, to do so. She also wrote *Madame Dorthea*,[15] the first volume of a projected novel she never completed; *Madame Dorthea* was her only historical novel set in the Age of Reason and in many respects it was her novel of farewell. Married young to an aged pastor, Dorthea finds fulfilment after his death as the wife of a successful glass-factory owner and bears him seven children. As the novel opens, however, her Jörgen is inexplicably lost in a storm and Dorthea has to face life alone, without even the certainty that he is dead. Like Julie Selmer, she flirts with the empty promise of spiritualism, and like Kristin, she is drawn to simple faith. The old Catholic worker Scharlach holds to a mystical belief in Divine Providence much like Brother Edvin's, but Dorthea rejects both seance and formal prayer. Carl Beyerschmidt notes that '[because] of her rationalistic mind Madame Dorthea sees a certain ambiguity in all religion and she is therefore reluctant to accept what she cannot logically understand' *Sigrid Undset*, pp. 151–2). Still, as Sigrid Undset's last fictional embodiment of her ideal of motherhood, Madame Dorthea clings to an unshakeable faith in God, and at the close of the novel old Scharlach, one of the few sympathetically drawn Germans in Sigrid Undset's work, reassures her: '. . . with your faith you will at any rate never be *altogether* unhappy (*Madame Dorthea*, p. 348).

Signe Undset Thomas believed that her sister had intended to round out her theme with a novel on the lives of Dorthea's sons, but in the autumn of 1939 Nazi lightning struck an unbelieving Europe. The North had once associated war's madness with the runes and rage of the Saxon god Norwegians named Odin; now as the Nazis ravaged Poland and Britain struggled with the eerie 'phoney war' Scandinavia watched in impotent dread. Sigrid Undset spent her last winter at Bjerkebaek for six years; it marked the end of her life as a creative artist.

Notes

1. Martin Seymour-Smith, *New Guide to Modern World Literature* (New York: Peter Bedrick, 1984), p. 1117.
2. A.H. Winsnes, *Sigrid Undset: A Study in Christian Realism*, trans. P.G. Foote (New York: Sheed and Ward, 1953), p. 194.
3. Alrik Gustafson, 'Christian Ethics in a Pagan World', in *Six Scandinavian Novelists* (Minneapolis, Minn.: University of Minnesota Press, 1968), p. 359.
4. Sigrid Undset, *The Bridal Wreath*, trans. Charles Archer and J.S. Scott (New York: Knopf, 1920: repr. Bantam,1978), p. 38.
5. Borghild Krane, *Sigrid Undset. Liv og meninger* (Oslo: Gyldendal, 1970), p. 54; my translation.
6. Sigrid Undset, *The Wild Orchid*, trans. Arthur G. Chater (New York: Knopf, 1931).
7. Idem, *The Burning Bush*, trans. Arthur G. Chater (New York: Knopf, 1933).

8. Idem, *Stages on the Road*, trans. Arthur G. Chater (New York: Knopf, 1934), p. 146.
9. Quoted in Carl Bayerschmidt, *Sigrid Undset* (New York: Twayne, 1970), p. 43.
10. Sigrid Undset, *Ida Elisabeth*, trans. Arthur G. Chater (New York: Knopf, 1933), p. 432.
11. Idem, *Saga of Saints*, trans. E.C. Ramsden. (New York: Knopf, 1937), p. 95.
12. Idem, *Men, Women and Places*, trans. Arthur G. Chater (New York: Knopf, 1939), p. 125.
13. Katharine Scherman, *The Flowering of Ireland* (Boston: Little, Brown, 1981), p. 16.
14. D.H. Lawrence, 'On Being Religious', *Adelphi*, February 1924; available more widely in *Phoenix: The Posthumous Papers of D.H. Lawrence*, ed. Edward MacDonald (New York: Viking Compass, 1936), pp. 724–30. Citation in text from p. 727.
15. Sigrid Undset, *Madame Dorthea*, trans. Arthur G. Chater (New York: Knopf, 1940).

8 Meetings and Partings: 1940–1949

> This I do in the sacred name of my country.
> Sigrid Undset

While the Nazi war machine gathered momentum in the 1930s, many Europeans deluded themselves, believing not only that Europe's interrelated economies made war impossible, but even, as Julie Selmer had said, that the socialists would surely stop any war that might begin: '. . . a soldier's strike would be declared immediately over the whole of Europe. . . . even now it [socialism] is a fairly secure guarantee of the world's peace' (*Wild Orchid*, p. 116).

Sigrid Undset knew better. She had distrusted elements in the German national character for a long time, from her father's untidy condescending colleague and the arrogant Prussians of the power company where she had worked to what she considered inconsistencies, if not heresies, in the teachings of Martin Luther. Even before Hitler became Chancellor of Germany in 1933, Sigrid Undset had begun to pit her formidable faith and relentless logic against the menace to Christianity she saw lurking in the Teutonic woods across the North Sea from Scandinavia.

In 1929 and 1930, the years of *The Wild Orchid* and *The Burning Bush*, Sigrid Undset also published two brief but significant Christmas meditations in German, 'Und wäre dies Kindlein nicht geboren?' ('And What If This Baby Were Not Born?') and 'Das Weihnachtswunder' ('The Christmas Miracle'). By stressing what A.H. Winsnes calls 'the paradoxical in Christianity', Sigrid Undset illustrated the gulf between Christian faith and pragmatism carried to extremes the world could not yet believe: '. . . if it is not ours, then what importance can a tiny baby have? Why not kill it if it is unwanted? . . . perhaps it will vitiate *die Kraft der Rasse?* . . . "there is no reason to answer this question in the negative, no reason except the whole of Christianity"'.[1]

In 1931, Sigrid Undset addressed the German people in *Begegnungen und Trennungen. Essays über Christentum und Germanentum* ('Meetings and Partings: Essays on Christianity and Germanism'), German versions of three of her most important reflections on history and psychology: 'Olaf der Heilige. Christentum und germanisches Naturheidentum' ('St Olaf: Christianity and Germanic Paganism'), which was originally published in 1930; 'Rückkehr zur katholischen Kirche' ('Return to the Catholic Church'), a translation of *Catholic Propaganda*, which had first appeared in 1927; and 'Christentum und Neuheidentum' ('Christianity and [the] New Paganism'), a translation of 'Letter to a Parish Priest', which had originally been printed in *Credo* in 1930.

Sigrid Undset's Introduction to *Begegnungen und Trennungen* reiterates her lifelong theme, humanity's yearning for a God to worship in joy as well as desperation. Far from condemning the old pagan reverence towards nature, Sigrid Undset accepted it as the basis for Scandinavia's conversion to Christianity, calling the old paganism: 'a love poem to a God who remained hidden, or . . . an attempt to gain the favour of the divine powers whose presence man felt about him' (quoted in Winsnes, *Sigrid Undset*, 215–16). She believed St Olaf built upon that natural impulse with Christian teachings which reinforced and reinvigorated the profound regard most Norwegians had for law and decency; men who trusted solely in human strength, like the pagan Lade Jarls of the North and even Erlend Nikulausson, could not accept the new God's salvation and perished. Although both St Olaf's time and her own were filled with people whose traditional faith had crumbled, Sigrid Undset sharply differentiated the old paganism from the new, which she considered 'a declaration of war against a God who has revealed himself' (ibid., p. 218). She could see only one recourse for twentieth-century man, and that was wholehearted affirmation of conservative Christian dogma: 'Sentimental clinging to . . . the individual parts of the Christian tradition is of no use at all. Break branches from a tree in the countryside and put them in vases to decorate your rooms — and see how long they stay fresh' (ibid., p. 218). Like European culture as a whole, she felt certain that German culture would expire if Germany rejected its Christian heritage, and more clearly than most of her contemporaries she recognised that Nazism, arisen out of Germany's materialistic *Weltanschauung*, foretold cultural suicide.

In the early 1930s, Adolf Hitler announced his own intention of 'eradicating Christianity in Germany down to the last root-fibre. Against the Christian teaching of the eternal worth of the individual soul and of personal responsibility, I declare, ruthlessly and with absolute definition, another doctrine of salvation ... the individual is insignificant, is nothing, compared to the immortality of the nation in this world'.[2] The Nazis had already enacted anti-Semitic laws in 1934, and the first trains began to arrive at Nazi concentration camps.

Sigrid Undset attacked Nazism directly for the first time in 'Fortschritt, Rasse, Religion' ('Progress, Race, Religion') in 1935, an essay that appeared in *Die Gefahrdung des Christentums durch Rassenwahn und Judenverfolgung* ('The Endangerment of Christianity through Race-Insanity and Persecution of the Jews'), a collection of articles by Protestants and Catholics published by the refugee firm Vita Nova in Lucerne. Sigrid Undset traced the development of modern graven images like technological progress, racial superiority and 'self-created' religion to the fatal pride of Lucifer, confronting both Nazism and Marxism on the moral ground where such doctrines are most vulnerable. She opposed totalitarianism with the Christian recognition of human frailty and reliance on Christ's offer of redemption to all men 'who ... give themselves to the belief in eternal life, and ... possess sufficient humility to seek the company of their Creator, rather than persisting in isolation and in service to fetishes, in the cult of ideas and things they have created for themselves ... since self-worship cannot stand by itself, it is the cult of the path toward dissolution and death'.[3]

Sigrid Undset had a wide audience in Germany. During the centennial of her birth, Heiko Uecker, Professor of Scandinavian Studies at the University of Bonn, observed that despite being added in 1929 by 'a conference of high priests of the arch-diocese of Breslau ... to the list of books which endangered the concept of Christian marriage' *Kristin Lavransdatter* had soon 'made its way to the top in Germany'. He further noted that Germans had consistently held Sigrid Undset's medieval novels of Norway in 'affectionate esteem'.[4] Her popularity caused the Nazis to denounce her viciously; in 1937 the *Westdeutscher Beobachter* declared: 'Her works shall no longer be found in German papers, German libraries, and German bookshops'. In a harsher blow, on 15 May 1937, the Norwegian Nazi newspaper *Fronten* described her position as 'not merely foreign and offensive to us — it is hostile', representing 'one of the most corrupting forces outside the State', i.e. the Catholic Church (quoted in Winsnes, *Sigrid Undset*, p. 219).

Genuine conflict came to Scandinavia in late November 1939, in the midst of the 'phoney war', when the Soviet Union attacked Finland. World sympathy, some supplies, and a few volunteers from Sweden and Norway reached the Finns during their gallant but fruitless four-month struggle. In *Return to the Future*, her wartime memoir, Sigrid Undset observed ruefully: 'Finland's fight for life first awakened some of us to a more nearly realistic view' of the world neutral Scandinavia had tried to shut out; 'But not enough of us, and too few of those who, first and foremost, should have been awake'.[5] She, at least, had no illusions about either the Nazis or the Russians. At the height of the Russian invasion of Finland, a few weeks before the Nazis assaulted Norway, she sent a short autobiographical statement to *Twentieth-Century Authors* with a prophetic note: 'I have always hated publicity about myself. But as things are looking here in Fenno-Scandia [sic] at present — we may all be swallowed up and deported somewhere in Siberia. . . . I have come to the conclusion that I may just as well tell something about myself whilst I can.'[6]

Sigrid Undset sold her Nobel Prize medal to aid the Finns, and in the spring of 1940 she took three Finnish refugee children into Bjerkebaek. In early April she went to Oslo to lecture at the same Student Union she had addressed twenty-six years earlier. On 9 April, as she was returning to Lillehammer, the Nazis invaded Norway. Outraged, she contributed what she could to the defence effort; she worked briefly as a censor, and her sons joined the Norwegian volunteers. Most of *Return to the Future* deals with her subsequent flight from the Nazis; she was President of the Norwegian Authors' Guild, and advised that she might be forced to make propaganda broadcasts — or worse — she left Lillehammer on 20 April. She reacted in a typically Norwegian fashion, with a passionate love for her country and an equally powerful revulsion at Nazi barbarism.

Throughout her exile, Sigrid Undset displayed an unusual outward detachment towards her personal tragedies. Charlotte Blindheim recalls that even though her aunt bitterly missed

Tulla, who had died in January 1939, Sigrid Undset was relieved that her daughter did not have to endure the war, and, in fact, she felt that Tulla's death had 'smoothed the way' to America for her.[7] Nevertheless the long trip to the New World was the most sorrowful of Sigrid Undset's many journeys.

Return to the Future (1942)

Nowhere in Sigrid Undset's work is Norway's beauty so poignantly drawn as it is in the first section of *Return to the Future*, 'Norway, Spring 1940'. Hoping to sail for England, she first travelled north with the Paasches, where a few Norwegians, with some British and French soldiers, were still holding out: '... every waking hour we all thought the same thing: that this our country, Norway, is so beautiful ... and it is ours, *ours*' (*Return to the Future*, p. 41). Along the way she might have thought of a famous passage from the *Njála*, the book she said had changed her life; as Gunnar takes leave of his farmstead Hlidarendi he suddenly bursts out: '"Fair is the hillside. It has never seemed so fair to me before ... I shall ride back home and never leave'.[8] Driven from Bjerkebaek at the age of fifty-eight, and physically weakened by a life of hard but largely sedentary work, Sigrid Undset could hardly 'ride back home and never leave'; she had not ski'd for twenty years, and when the Nazis closed off the northern sea route from Tromsø, she had to be hauled across the mountains to Sweden on a sled pulled by strong young men.

Far greater pain was waiting; in May, Sigrid Undset learned that her oldest son Anders, aged twenty-seven, had died on 26 April with his machine-gun unit defending Segalstad Bridge, not far from Lillehammer. Anders, trained for four years as an engineer in England and engaged to be married, had also possessed the Norwegian restraint with which his mother now mourned him. She recalled in *Return to the Future* that one of Anders' men had visited her in Stockholm, describing Anders as 'an incomparably kind person', and she mused, '*Snill* — the untranslatable Norwegian word; *kind* comes nearest to it, but *snilhet* must be quiet in manner, undemonstrative ... for most Norwegians the best that can be said of a person is that he is *snill*' (ibid., p. 72). She thanked God, she told her Swedish friends, with France falling and the British Army evacuating Dunkirk and the West seeming soon to be engulfed in *Götterdämmerung*, 'that Anders does not have to experience this' (ibid., p. 66). Charlotte Blindheim believes that Anders' death was a blow which Sigrid Undset 'bore with admirable outward calm, but never really got over'.[9]

Sigrid Undset waited in Stockholm until late May, when her last child, Hans, could join her. He had been working in a medical unit, but after an interview with the Gestapo he had simply taken a train to one of Norway's forest provinces and walked through the woods to Sweden. He had seen Nazi atrocities, like violations of Red Cross conventions and executions of Norwegian civilians, but he and his mother were aghast at the Nazis' treatment of their own soldiers. The Norwegians fought 'silent as the mountains', but Sigrid Undset attributed 'the abominable bellowing' of advancing Germans to cocaine-laced chocolate given them before a battle. She and Hans were revolted by the grubby German nurses and the 'sad human specimens' of ordinary German soldiers, 'bowlegged, narrow-shouldered, flat-footed individuals, with broad, drooping bottoms. . . . Probably no particularly magnificent physique is needed for . . . operating machines for mass slaughter' (*Return to the Future*, p. 78).

Norwegian and Allied troops did recapture Narvik on 29 May, Germany's first defeat in the war, but the Allies decided to withdraw immediately afterward. Norway surrendered on 9 June, and although Sigrid Undset had hoped for a miracle to save France, 'the motherland of ideas of good and evil which had always been fruitful in Scandinavian intellectual life and Scandinavian art' (ibid., p. 79), France fell two weeks later. 'It had to be America', for Sigrid Undset and her son. On 13 July they flew from Stockholm to Moscow; from there they would take the Trans-Siberian Express to Vladivostok, and then sail to Japan, boarding the *President Cleveland* at Kobe for San Francisco.

Under the best circumstances the trip would have been daunting, but in the summer of 1940 Sigrid Undset knew she was a Christian face to face with evil. Stalin still felt secure in his pact with Hitler, anticipating the spoils of Eastern Europe, and Japan had invaded Manchuria in 1937, setting up a Chinese puppet regime at Nanking in 1940. Sigrid Undset needed all her hard-headed practicality and her grim Northern humour to survive.

Arriving in Moscow, she wrote, was like dropping 'from the skies into another world', all the glorious Communist slogans amounting to 'indescribable filth, dilapidation, wretchedness' (ibid., p. 133). Sigrid Undset and Hans endured Moscow's 'overpowering stench' and then sat 'still . . . getting dirtier and dirtier' for nine days across Siberia without water to wash in. She pungently observed the lethal totalitarian similarities between National Socialism and Communism, in particular the Nazi and Soviet population theories that intentionally defied hygienic principles so that only the strongest would survive to support the state. At the time she also was virtually alone in calling attention not only to 'rumors of systematic murder of the weak, sick, or defective individuals' in Germany, but also to 'a deeper misery and human suffering' beneath the noisome surface of Soviet existence, the ironclad prison cars feeding vast numbers of men, women and children into Stalin's Gulag. By the time she reached Vladivostok, a city whose vermin defied even her formidable powers of description, Sigrid Undset's perception of Communism focused on one small victim that summed up the tragedy of the entire country, a dying tubercular girl who remined her of Tulla: 'Next to the glimpse into the hell of the prison train Oleha was the worst I saw in Soviet Russia' (*Return to the Future*, p. 141).

Although the cleanliness of Japan must have been a blessed relief, Sigrid Undset gradually discovered disturbing evidence that Japan was also a ruthless country at war, although she 'was expected to trip along behind the youth [Hans] and keep silent' (ibid., p. 155). The stores had nothing but artificial silk, because the real material all went for parachutes: 'German trash, cheap and hideous' was in all the shop windows; and most alarming, the Japanese were even short of their staple food, rice. For Sigrid Undset, this exemplified the universal rule basic to totalitarian societies: 'the standard of living sinks surely and steadily . . . and the only method which the rulers know of attaining the promised land for their people is to conquer neighboring countries' (ibid., p. 174). It is less a measure of Sigrid Undset's perspicacity than of Western naïvety that so few heeded her warning about that deadly common denominator of totalitarian systems — as, indeed, few do today.

From the very first, Sigrid Undset believed that the road back to the future could lead only across America. From 26 August

1940, when she landed in San Francisco, until she returned to Lillehammer five years later, Arne Skouen, who in 1944 became Director of the Norwegian Information Service in the United States, described her as 'a Norwegian soldier behind a typewriter'. She crisscrossed the USA on lecture tours, and in the Midwest she was 'frequently reminded in a strange way' of her grandparents' world when she attended 'social functions among Norwegian Americans or read American newspapers in the Norwegian language'. Such experiences made her think, she said, of pressed flowers in an album, because the Norwegian–Americans preserved the language and culture 'of a Norway that people of my age recalled only faintly from childhood'.[10]

She was also writing almost continuously — radio scripts, book reviews for the *New York Times*, articles in support of the Norwegian Resistance and hundreds of news items for the Norwegian Information Service; Arne Skouen declared that 'it was partly due to her efforts when President Franklin Delano Roosevelt made his historic statement of 1942, appraising America's allies among the occupied countries, naming a gallant example: look to Norway!'[11]

The title essay of *Return to the Future* contains the crux of Sigrid Undset's anti-totalitarian message. Her experiences in 1940 had confirmed what she had been announcing for nearly a decade, that totalitarian systems devour victims both within and outside their national borders; if Nazism and Communism could expand their spheres of influence through the subversion of the Western democracies they would, but as events had shown, they would even undertake wars of domination, reducing captive peoples and their own populations to a subhuman existence denying man's need for God. As Britain fought on alone, before the Japanese attack on Pearl Harbor brought the USA into the war on 7 December 1941, Sigrid Undset believed that nothing less than the future of Western civilisation was at stake. She insisted that the two world wars were stages of the same conflict between two incompatible concepts of life; in the First World War, 'nations who had never had any leanings toward the democratic pattern' had attempted to halt the march of democracy, while in 1941 'nations like Germany were desperately attempting to destroy democracy completely' ('Norway and Norwegian Americans', p. 76).

From her lifelong moral viewpoint, too, an even greater danger loomed. If the West acted out of hatred and revenge, passions she considered sterile and self-destructive, democracy could win the war but lose its soul to totalitarianism. 'How in God's name', she asked out of a mother's grief and an exile's outrage, 'will it be possible to neutralize that hate which consumes all the victims of Germany's lying and faithlessness, German sadism, German rapaciousness and greed . . . so that it does not completely paralyze all constructive forces in the peoples?' (*Return to the Future*, p. 211).

Sigrid Undset answered as a practising Catholic must, in God's name, but her very question reveals that she experienced the same painful emotions she felt Germany's victims had to overcome in order to survive spiritually. On this rare occasion her logic fails to convince, because her righteous wrath at Nazi *Schweinerei* disrupts her sense of equilibrium. She carried to an indefensible extreme her insistence that 'by no means the whole [Scandinavian people] . . . roved as vikings' (ibid., p. 211), claiming that the crews of the dragon ships from whose fury Europe prayed for a thousand years to be delivered 'were in large part farm boys who made some expeditions before they settled down in peace' (ibid., p. 212), while at the same time condemning Germany's entire cultural history: 'Nazi Germany's peculiarities . . . have been traits in the psychology of the German people since time immemorial, which Nazism has brought into the full light of day' (ibid., p. 225).

In Christian charity, Sigrid Undset also insisted that Germany's national aberration deserved medical treatment, because its people were 'constitutionally unpeaceful, spiteful, obsessed by grudges against real or imagined antagonists . . . [that is] every single person with whom they come into more than the most passing contact' (ibid., p. 234). In the dark months of 1941, she felt German conquests had sprung from their unhealthy desire to be mastered; German honour out of someone else's death; German art out of diseases of body and soul. Under the pressures of fatigue, exile, justifiable anger and an unassuageable grief for her son and her home, Sigrid Undset's great art was dissolving into propaganda, the greatest sacrifice she could have made for the war effort. Even in the essay 'Return to the Future', one of her most fervent anti-German works, she said she clung to the

Roman Catholic moral defences of faith, hope and love, and 'our own exertions . . . tireless, patient, and courageous exertion' (*Return to the Future*, p. 251), but her labours took their toll. The ageing woman wracked by a chronic bronchial ailment who longed to go home to Lillehammer was far from the robust, serious-minded Norwegian artist who had left it.

When Arne Skouen joined the Norwegian Information Service in 1944, he found Sigrid Undset living in two modest annexe rooms of the Hotel Margaret in Brooklyn, 'a Nobel Prize winner who told me that she was nothing but an old woman reporter'. He perceived that she was marked by 'the refugee's particular kind of loneliness . . . [all that] kept her in working shape . . . [was] her long wanderings and her friendships'. Skouen also recalled that she avoided the 'literary set of distinguished emigrés like Thomas Mann and others' but 'she sought and found friendships among Americans . . . far away from the mainstream' (Skouen, 'The Nobel Prize Laureate', pp. 3–6). She became close to the social reformer Dorothy Day and to Hope Emily Allen, an authority on medieval mysticism; and she developed deep friendships with Willa Cather, whose work she admired, and Marjorie Kinnan Rawlings, author of *The Yearling*, a tender story of childhood. Sigrid Undset also met Jacques Maritain, the French neothomist philosopher whose work had inspired her for a long time.

Buttressing all of Sigrid Undset's wartime activities was her immense concern for the future, embodied in the children of the world whom she addressed in *Happy Times in Norway*, 1942, and *Sigurd and his Brave Companions*, 1943, two of her three books published during the war, as well as *True and Untrue and Other Norse Tales*, 1945, her edition of the Asbjørnson–Moe collection. The relation of mother and child had always been the keystone of her art as well as her life, and when she came home to Norway, Charlotte Blindheim observes that the full import of her maternal loss struck Sigrid Undset as it never had before: 'She didn't fully realize it [Anders' death] until she returned to Bjerkebaek in July of 1945, to a home bereft of two children. The house had been inhabited by the Germans since 1942. In a way we think this broke her' (*Scandinavian Review*, p. 54).

Postwar conditions in Norway were miserable. Sigrid Undset noted in a letter to her American friend Mrs Alf Jorgen Stromsted dated 30 October 1945 that in the north the Germans had killed the cattle, sunk the fishing boats and burned 60,000 homes. In Lillehammer food was severely rationed, and Sigrid Undset caught a bronchial infection that was never really cured. The Nazis had destroyed her father's writing desk where she had written all of her greatest work, and even the gold lace and velvet dress she had worn to the Nobel ceremony in Stockholm had vanished, traded by her sister Signe for a bread knife (*Moster Sigrid*, p. 75). According to Margaret Mary Dunn, Borghild Krane observed: 'Living alone at Bjerkebaek to which her only living son Hans hardly ever came, she had lots of time to assess her life. . . . She worried about the things she had sacrificed because she had prioritized others, and was plagued with shame at . . . how often she had defended her standpoints on life's problems with unyielding intensity, even anger'. An American, a former nun and a scholar of Sigrid Undset's works, Margaret Mary Dunn agreed with Borghild Krane that towards the last, Sigrid Undset wanted to sell Bjerkerbaek and return to Oslo, 'to mingle with people and become immersed in Norwegian-American affairs', but she lacked the 'physical and psychic strength to live differently'.[12]

On her sixty-fifth birthday, 20 May 1947, Sigrid Undset received Norway's highest honour, the Grand Cross of the Order of Saint Olaf, the first woman after Crown Princess Martha to do so. Given as much for Sigrid Undset's service to Norway as for her literary achievements, St Olaf's Cross also symbolised her special holocaust, the renunciation of her art for her country. In one of her last articles, 'Abraham's Sacrifice', she wryly commented: '. . . human beings are always architects of their own misfortune, and . . . they always forget with equal rapidity, every instance of God's mercy. . . . I can discover nothing in the history of the world, from the legendary past to the present day, which is capable of disproving this conviction' (quoted in Winsnes, *Sigrid Undset*, p. 245).

The enervation of the postwar world depressed and saddened her. On 20 December 1948, she wrote to her fellow Norwegian author Hans Aanrud: '. . . neither did I expect "the new age" to be so anemic and feeble, though with so much blood spilled it is not strange people should suddenly give the impression of being anemic, rebellious, and unenterprising'.[13] She struggled to complete her biography of Catherine of Siena, the late fourteenth-century Dominican reformer, but the publisher Doubleday's rejection of it shortly before her death must have seemed cruel confirmation that hers now was, in Yeats' phrase, an 'outworn heart in a time outworn'. On 10 June 1949 she died alone in the hospital at Hamar, the medieval bishop's seat that had held forgiveness so close and yet so far beyond Olav Audunsson's grasp. For her family, Charlotte Blindheim says, Sigrid Undset's death 'was like having a solid anchor cut away' (*Scandinavian Review*, p. 54), and so it must have been for Norway; the author who had brought two thousand years of Norway's history to life was gone. At her funeral in Hamar, her king and country gave her all the honours they had to give, laying her to rest between Anders and Tulla in the Mesnalien Cemetery near Lillehammer, with a grave marker that declares her to be, like Kristin Lavransdatter, 'a loyal handmaiden of the Lord'.

Notes

1. Quoted in A.H. Winsnes, *Sigrid Undset: A Study in Christian Realism* trans. P.G. Foote (New York: Sheed and Ward, 1953), p. 215.
2. From the Preface to Edmond Vermeil's *Hitler et le Christianisme* (London: 1944), quoted in ibid., p. 218
3. Sigrid Undset, 'Fortschrift, Rasse, Religion' ('Progress, Race, Religion'), in *Die Gefährdung des Christenums durch Rassenwahn und Judenverfolgung* ('The Endangerment of Christianity through Race-Insanity and Persecution of the Jews') (Lucerne, Switzerland: Vita Nova Verlag, 1935). My translation.
4. Heiko Uecker, 'Sigrid Undset and Germany', unpublished paper supplied by the Norwegian Information Service in the United States (see 'Bibliographical Notes'), p. 8.
5. Sigrid Undset, *Return to the Future*, trans. Henriette C.K. Naeseth (New York: Knopf, 1942), pp. 6–7.
6. Stanley J. Kunitz and Howard Haycroft (eds.), *Twentieth Century Authors* (New York: H.W. Wilson, 1942; 7th printing, 1973), p. 1,434.
7. Charlotte Blindheim, *Moster Sigrid: Et familie portrett au Sigrid Undset* (Oslo: Aschehoug, 1982), p. 8; cited as *Moster Sigrid*.
8. Peter Hallberg, *The Icelandic Saga*, trans. Paul Schach (Lincoln, Nebraska: University of Nebraska Press, 1962), p. 155.
9. Blindheim, *Moster Sigrid*; translated in an excerpt published in *The*

Scandinavian Review, vol. 70, no. 2 (June 1982), p. 54.

10. Sigrid Undset, 'Norway and Norwegian Americans', Common Ground (1940–2), pp. 74–5.

11. Arne Skouen, 'The Nobel Prize Laureate who Loved Brooklyn Bridge', unpublished paper supplied by the Norwegian Information Service in the United States, 1982, pp. 3–6.

12. Quoted from Borghild Krane, Sigrid Undset in M.M. Dunn, 'Sigrid Undset Seen Through the Eyes of An American Woman Religious', unpublished paper supplied by the Norwegian Information Service, p. 10.

13. Quoted in Carl Bayerschmidt, Sigrid Undset (New York: Twayne, 1970), p. 53.

9 Another Life: Sigrid Undset's Achievements

One thing I know that never dies,
The fame of a dead man's deeds.
Hávamál

In art, as in everything else, Sigrid Undset had no patience with overbearing dilettantes: in a letter dated 30 October 1945 to Mrs Stromsted, Sigrid Undset commented:

> . . . those who are poor or half-poor artists and lady artists are the most demanding and most convinced of their own right to bother other people "in the name of art". Those that really are [artists] are usually so sure of themselves that they are in reality ordinary natural people, but those who are struggling with secret misgivings about their own ability become nuisances to themselves and for everyone else who gets in their way . . . [my translation].

As both artist and 'ordinary' woman, Sigrid Undset herself lived by many of the commonsense rules suggested in the Old Norse *Hávamál* ('Sayings of the Wise One'): to venerate the home and respect the mutual obligations of guest and host; to approach friendships cautiously, but to give them with the whole heart; to uphold the virtues of hard work and finally enjoy the reward of fame, 'the word that lives on when a man is gone'.[1] Very little in Sigrid Undset's life came easily, and her works are not widely read today; much of her contemporary literary acclaim has slipped away, just as many conservative Roman Catholic views melted in the aftermath of the Second Vatican Council. Nevertheless, Sigrid Undset's pre-eminent position in Scandinavian realistic literature endures, and her matchless recreations of medieval Norway ensure *Kristin Lavransdatter* and *The Master of Hestviken* a permanent place among the world's literary masterpieces.

Sigrid Undset's German contemporary Rainer Maria Rilke called artists who create such work 'the lonely ones', and no name could better describe the price a woman must pay for her art. She

125

must wrench time to create her glimpses of the Eternal Now from the endless demands of wife- and motherhood in the here and now that stretches from birth to grave, and as well as the painful isolation the male artist feels from 'the bright children of life, the happy, the charming and the ordinary',[2] from whom their art, like Tonio Kröger's, forever separates them, the woman artist bears the guilt of neglecting her family in order to write, paint, or make music. Only a few women — and Sigrid Undset was one — accept art's loneliness and its pain as the cost of creations that never match their dreams.

All of Sigrid Undset's work rests on the cornerstone of her integrity; to the end she kept faith with the truth that she paid so dearly to learn. Even more than her few autobiographical statements, her general comments on Scandinavian literature, produced in the 1940s, reveal the core of her art: a relentless realism that enfolds the certainty of man's salvation — provided he submits himself to the authority of Almighty God. That message, unpopular in our time, is not bound to hers; it is one more reminder that if man does not heed the lessons of the past he will be doomed to repeat them.

In 1939, Sigrid Undset wrote: 'The [First World] war and the years afterwards confirmed the doubts I always had had about the ideas I was brought up on — [I felt] that liberalism, feminism, nationalism, socialism, pacifism, would not work, because they refused to consider human nature as it really is'.[3] She believed that a constant of human behaviour is unconscious or subconscious 'spontaneous admiration of conquerors and men of violence' who seek to dominate men's souls, and that 'to fight these would-be masters of men' (ibid., p. 1,433), the only efficacious weapons are spiritual ones: '. . . there can never be any valid authority of men over men. The only Authority to which mankind can submit without debauching itself is His . . . the Creator's toward Creation' (ibid., p. 1,434).

In her 1943 lecture 'Scandinavian Literature',[4] she implicitly defined her place in the Northern literary tradition which had paradoxically combined realism and idealism for centuries. She began where her heart had dwelt so constantly since Tulla's and Anders' deaths, with 'the vivid thumbnail sketches of children' that crowd the Icelandic sagas and Snorri Sturluson's portraits of two Norwegian princes. Sigrid Undset claimed her nation's

200-year path from the Viking Age to the height of Christian governance was represented by two extremes: St Olaf as an arrogant bull-headed boy and the 'almost too angelic' Haakon Haakonsson, who set 'our laws and customs . . . among the most just and humane in Europe' ('Scandinavian Literature', pp. 1–2).

Sigrid Undset saw the Scandinavian mentality as essentially separate from European traditions. She believed that Scandinavian minds rejected both French 'cynicism for its own sake' and German 'sadistic wallowings in the sufferings of the heroes'; she admitted Scandinavians and Germans shared an ancient common ancestry, but 'the family likeness had disappeared entirely in the twelfth century' (ibid., p. 4) — so much for Hitler's claims of Germanic solidarity. She felt certain that the Northern personality was most at home with the sagas' 'realistic and penetrating sense of human nature' (ibid., p. 3), which, though it became the chief literary characteristic of Scandinavia as a whole, was for Sigrid Undset specifically Norway's reaction to the nineteenth-century German Romantic Movement, in which poets pursued Novalis' 'Blaue Blume', the mystical goal of the neoplatonic artist separated by his gifts from the rest of humanity.

Whereas in Sweden and Denmark nineteenth-century writers responded by celebrating their forefathers' independence — 'No man's masters, no man's slaves' — Sigrid Undset believed that Norway's own struggle for independence generated an entirely different reaction to Romanticism in the first modern Norwegian psychological novel, dealing with the lives of the oppressed — and, she noted, it was significant that it was written by a woman, Camilla Collett. By the time Norwegian social conditions began to improve, Norwegian writers approached naturalism with Jonas Lie's 'ruthless sincerity' and Amalie Skram's preoccupation with the 'frightening and sinister force' of sex (ibid., p. 11). One keynote stands out both in Sigrid Undset's analysis of Norway's literature and in all of her own work: 'Life, even at its saddest and most tragic, is still worth while — worth while living and a worthy material to create art from . . .' (ibid., p. 14).

Nothing less than the value of life dominates Sigrid Undset's fiction. All of her books resound with the greatest sorrows human beings can bear, the self-made torments that result from broken vows and choices made too soon only to be repented at painful leisure. Yet not one of her books ends without the promise of hope, as much a clue to her personality as to her art. Very late in her life, Sigrid Undset revealed that as an author she found it easier to identify with people quite different from herself, so that the 'family likeness' between herself and her characters went so deep it could be discerned often only accidentally.[5] Unconscious revelations, however, are generally more accurate than an author's conscious choices; and Charlotte Blindheim remarks that 'since we apprehend her books as realistic, written from her own experience or action, it makes us who have known her read her books in our own way, we always look for her part'.[6]

Most of Sigrid Undset's commentators agree that the woman who chose to live in old Norwegian farmhouses, wearing the heavy wool skirts and richly embroidered blouses of her native costume at home, collecting plants and old lace, 'recreated history by reliving it in her mind' (Beyer, 'Sigrid Undset', p. 307). Her literary reputation today rests almost entirely on *Kristin Lavransdatter* and *The Master of Hestviken*, novels which bring Norway's fourteenth century to life, but most readers find her powerful psychological portraiture far more affecting than her painstakingly accurate historical reconstructions. Sigrid Undset gave her people eternal life; Kristin and Olav, Lavrans and Erlend and Ingunn walk forever on Norway's heights and through the valleys of their individual shadows, impossible to forget.

The evidence of her fiction confirms her own conviction that the *Njála* she read at eleven had made a turning-point in Sigrid Undset's life, since it voiced the theme she never abandoned as an artist: that the individual must bear the responsibility of his actions. She believed that human responsibility rested chiefly on the basic relationship of the family, and she focused on the feminine role as few writers have been able to do, having lived it to an intense degree. In her early work, she refused to blame society for women's problems as her predecessors had done, and she would have had no patience with modern feminist claims that male domination has prevented women's achievements; rather she insisted on women's biological, emotional and rational differences from men, stressing women's primal need for fulfilment in their marriages and their children, though she also acknowledged women's need to realise their potential in other roles, the crux of women's problems that remain unresolved today. When her own first child was born, Charlotte Blindheim had to tell her redoubtable aunt that she intended to return to her job, 'the best in the whole country', and to remind Moster Sigrid that '. . . you had done the same, only you had your work at home and the children did not have permission to disturb you'. Mrs Blindheim recalls taking a firm grip on her courage, saying: 'What you want to say now, Aunt Sigrid, is that, "But I am Sigrid Undset"'. Sigrid Undset agreed; but Mrs Blindheim feels that her aunt would not have approved her giving her job up either (*Moster Sigrid*, p. 97). For Sigrid Undset, as many of her essays and stories indicate, the contradictions of a gifted woman's lot demanded sacrifices beyond most men's endurance.

Sigrid Undset visited soon again after the baby was born, and Charlotte Blindheim asked the question in the mind of every woman who reads *Kristin Lavransdatter*: '"Aunt Sigrid, was it necessary to portray the birth scene in Kristin so realistically? Have you thought how many young pregnant women you have frightened?" She laughed and answered, "Yes, but Charlotte, that is the way it is"'. Mrs Blindheim believes the remark 'that is the way it is' is the most significant clue to her aunt's writing (ibid., p. 58).

Although her frank presentations of female sexuality may seem restrained today, Sigrid Undset was one of the first European authors to claim that women's need for physical satisfaction was as great and as justifiable as men's, though utterly dissimilar in nature. The concept which for her underlay the sexual equality of men and women was the vow that they exchanged: a Scandinavian warrior or an Oslo engineer might stray for physical release, but his wife could remain secure in her role in his life if each took their mutual bond seriously — and knew that the other did. On the other hand, Sigrid Undset felt a mother had to be unquestionably faithful; the primeval necessity of protecting the clan through the purity of its mothers illustrated mankind's one absolute law throughout history, and with her 1914 novel *Vaaren* ('Spring'), the archetypal season of birth, she began to emphasise a woman's choice of the maternal role over the marital and the conflicts the choice may bring.

By drawing closer to Roman Catholicism through acquaintance with its saints, men and women who to her 'seemed to know the true explanation of man's undying hunger for happiness — his tragically insufficient love of peace, justice, and goodwill . . .

129

his everlasting fall from grace' (*Twentieth Century Authors*, p. 1,433), Sigrid Undset found a new dimension for her fiction, the spiritual realm which counterpoints the realism of *Kristin Lavransdatter* and *The Master of Hestviken*. She deplored 'such a hubbub of praise for Kristin' (*Moster Sigrid*, p. 58), and she considered Olav Audunsson's story her greatest novel. Several critics disagree, seeing *The Master of Hestviken* as the forerunner of her fictional insistence on neothomist answers to the social and psychological problems of modern life, and some, like Alrik Gustafson, cite 'a distinct falling off in the quality' of her last works because of their heavy emphasis on Catholic dogma.

Charlotte Blindheim attests to her aunt's respect for the personal integrity of the members of her family; Sigrid Undset never tried to force her own beliefs upon them. On the other hand, Mrs Blindheim also notes that Sigrid Undset's uncompromising attacks on Norway's Lutheran establishment offended people, even those closest to her, and that her aunt was well aware that her own pride, which she called her greatest sin, caused her enormous difficulties (ibid., pp. 72–3). Even her most unsympathetic commentators, however, praise Sigrid Undset's sincerity; she assailed not only Norwegian social conditions but the dangerous materialism and sentimental humanitarianism that she felt threatened all of Western civilisation.

During the Second World War, Sigrid Undset fought harder than she ever had before to defend the values she thought that the Church had preserved for Europe. Now one Germany faces another over a wall erected by another form of totalitarianism, one whose aims Sigrid Undset had also identified long before the rest of the world would listen. Today her anti-German polemics may seem jingoistic and her celebrations of Scandinavian decency and 'beautiful America', as she called her place of exile, no more than dreams of a return to a future that may never exist, as she sadly discovered at the last, knowing that she had given up her literary work for wartime propaganda. It was the final bitter sacrifice of her life — realising that in the technological view of history, as its father Herodotus said, man can only step into the same river once.

This explains the wide difference between her greatest achievements, her two medieval novels, and her other fiction, which merits respect for her honest portrayal of individual entrances and exits on history's scene, the individual conquests of self that achieve human worth. But *Kristin Lavransdatter* and *The Master of Hestviken* transcend all her other work because they unflinchingly convey those deep mythic experiences which lie beyond rational explanation, experiences that only humanity's 'lonely ones' can live and transmit — myth as eternal truth.

Under the fearful pressures of the early twentieth century, its greatest authors, such as Lawrence, Joyce, Eliot, Rilke, and Thomas Mann, drew upon the context of the Eternal Now, when humanity relives in its religious impulse those moments when it greets the Divine. The intellectual explanations which dominate Sigrid Undset's later novels cannot plumb the profound human experiences of love and loyalty and the need of a God to worship, truths that have roots in man's innermost being, which she explores in *Kristin Lavransdatter* and *The Master of Hestviken*. She could best treat those matters of her own soul at the medieval crossroads of two cultures and two religions, whose conflicts supply the animating tension of her finest work. Sigrid Undset chose to set her greatest works in the moment when the Old Norse myths were giving way to the Myth of Christ, myth in its widest and most sacred sense. The sanctity of vows and the reverent urge of procreation that the pagans of the North worshipped as attributes of Thor and Freja, and the *beserker* rage and the dangerous irrationality of poetry that they believed Odin inspired all took their places in the new story of the Warrior who overcame Sin and Death once and for all time, and Sigrid Undset affirmed that sacrifice as central to the life of each Christian. Sigrid Undset's *Kristin Lavransdatter* and *The Master of Hestviken* drew her an artist's eternal life from the well of Norway's past, for all time confirming her profound conviction that 'life after all is a wonderful thing'.

Notes

1. Harald Beyer, 'Sigrid Undset', in Einar Haugen (ed.), *A History of Norwegian Literature*, trans. Einar Haugen (New York: New York University Press, 1956), p. 18.

2. Thomas Mann, *Tonio Kröger and Other Stories*, trans. David Luke (New York: Bantam, 1970), p. 217.

3. Stanley J. Kunitz and Howard Haycroft (eds.), *Twentieth Century Authors* (New York: H.W Wilson, 1942; 7th printing, 1973), p. 1433.

4. Sigrid Undset, 'Scandinavian Literature', *Quarterly Bulletin of the Polish Institute of Arts and Sciences in America* (July 1943).

5. Borghild Krane, *Sigrid Undset. Liv og meniger* (Oslo: Gyldendal, 1970), pp. 292–5.

6. Charlotte Blindheim, *Moster Sigrid. Et familie portrett av Sigrid Undset* (Oslo: Aschehoug, 1982), p. 59; this and subsequent references are my translations.

Chronology

I. *Early Norwegian History*

c. 3000 BC   Interior of Norway is settled and agriculture begins to develop.

1500–500 BC   Norwegian social organisation is evidenced by Bronze Age burial mounds.

c. A.D. 100   Tacitus' *Germania* describes culture of Germanic tribes.

300–600   Events recorded in Germanic works such as the *Volsungasaga* occur during Germanic expansion throughout Europe.

453   Attila the Hun is supposedly murdered on his wedding night.

?late 500s   Arthur leads British Celts against Saxon invaders of England.

?late 600s   *Beowulf* is composed.

The Viking Age: *c*. 850–*c*. 1100

Skalds orally compose complex poetry involving mythological tales and Viking exploits; the runic alphabet is used for magical lore; Christianity begins its long process of converting Scandinavia.

700s–800s   Norway is divided into about 29 *fylker*, each ruled by its own king.

c. 866   South-east (Vestfold) districts are united under Halfdan the Black of the Uppsala Yngling dynasty.

Harold Fairhair
(872–933) *
872   Halfdan's son Harold defeats rivals at Battle of Hafsfjord, confiscates their lands and unifies Norway; rival Viking lords settle in Iceland rather than submit to Harold's rule.

930   Harold divides Norway among 20 of his sons, with Erik Bloodaxe as over-king.

---

*The dates ascribed to each ruler apply to the duration of his reign, not his life.

Erik Bloodaxe (930–4)

Skalds begin to arrive in Norway from Iceland; the *Voluspå* ('The Sibyl's Prophecy') is created at Erik's court; Erik slays several brothers.

933   Harold Fairhair dies.

934   Erik is ejected from Norway by his brother Haakon Haroldsson.

Haakon I. Haroldsson the Good (935–61)

Haakon, brought up at the English court of Athelstan, attempted but failed to introduce Christianity to Norway, though he built up the Norwegian army and navy.

961   Haakon dies in battle against a group of Erikssons and their Danish allies.

Harold II Eriksson Greycloak (961–70)

970   Harold, who held only the western districts of Norway firmly, is killed by Earl Haakon Sigurdsson of Lade, grandson of Erik Bloodaxe. Haakon held the North with help of Danish allies.

Earl Haakon Sigurdsson (970–95)

Haakon was the last completely pagan ruler of Norway; he gathered skalds around him, threw off his Danish alliance, disregarded the landed aristocracy (*lendermaend*) and thereby caused revolt.

991   Battle of Maldon, occasion of greatest battle poem in English language; Earl Byrhtnoth of Essex is killed by Viking raiders, possibly including Olaf Tryggvasson.

Olaf I Tryggvasson (995–1000)

Olaf, great-grandson of Harold Fairhair, enforces conversion to Christianity, makes peace with England, and sends Leif Eriksson to spread the faith to Greenland and North America.

997   Olaf founds Nidaros (now Trondheim), political and religious capital of medieval Norway.

c. 1000   The Latin alphabet is introduced to Norway by missionary monks.

1000   Olaf falls in naval Battle of Solder against the Danes and the Swedes, who divide Norway; real power is held by Earls Erik and Svein Haakonsson.

Erik and Svein Haakonsson (1000–16)

Olaf II Haroldsson the Fat (Saint Olaf) (1016–29)

1016   Olaf defeats Earl Svein Haakonsson at Nesje. He establishes Norwegian Church; he attempts to unify Norway, but he antagonises nobles by appointing low-born men faithful to himself as court officials, and when Knut the Great of Denmark asserts his claim to Norway, the nobles defect.

1028   The nobles rebel against Olaf.

1029   Olaf flees to Russia, and Knut the Great claims Norway.

Svein Knutsson (1030–5)

1030   Olaf returns from exile and dies at Battle of Stiklestad against Svein, whose ferocious rule makes the name 'Saint Olaf' symbolic in Norway of freedom from foreign domination and the goal of internal union.

Magnus I Olafsson the Good (1035–47)

1035   Magnus is summoned from Russia; makes treaty with King of Denmark, where he also rules from 1042 to 1047; Magnus' rule leads to Norwegian decline and civil disorder until 1066.

Harold III Hardrade (1047–66)

A skald himself and half-brother to St Olaf, Harold dies at Stamford Bridge attempting to seize England from Harold Godwinson.

Olaf III Haroldsson the Quiet (1066–93) and *Magnus II Haroldsson (1066–9)*

During this period of relative peace, towns become increasing important in Norway; Bergen is founded.

The Age of the Sagas *c.* 1100–*c.* 1350

As Christianity becomes more widespread in Norway, skalds are increasingly unable to reconcile their poetic gift from the pagan god Odin, celebrating pagan warrior values, with the new faith. The Icelanders begin to write sagas, long prose narratives in intensely realistic style, about events from the earliest times in Scandinavia to the close of the Viking Age. Ballads, hymns, and translations of European courtly romances begin to replace skaldic verse.

Magnus III Olafsson the Barefoot (1093–1103) and *Haakon Magnusson (1093–5)*

1103   Magnus, having been defeated by Swedish King Inge at Battle of Foxerne in 1101, dies on third expedition to Scotland.

Olaf IV Magnusson (1103–16)   Sigurd I Magnusson Jorsalfar (1103–30)
Eystein I Magnusson (1103–22)

1130   Last of the three joint Magnusson rulers and the last undisputed representative of Harold Fairhair's line, Sigurd Jorsalfar dies insane. He had gone on a pilgrimage to Jerusalem, raided the Moors in Spain, defeated Mediterranean pirates, and with Baldwin I of Jerusalem took and sacked Sidon.

Magnus IV Sigurdsson (1130–5)

1133   Icelanders begin writing sagas.

1135   Magnus ousted by Harold Gille, who claims to be the illegitimate son of Magnus the Barefoot.

Harold IV Gille (Gilchrist) (1135–6)

1136   Harold is killed by another pretender to the throne, and Harold's three sons rule jointly

Sigurd II Haroldsson Mund (1136–55)
Eystein II (1136–57)
Inge I (1136–61)

1140–50   Nicholas Breakspear, who ruled from 1154 to 1159 as Pope Adrian IV (the only Englishman ever elected), organises Norwegian Church hierarchy.

1151   Only significant Norwegian-born skald, Ragnvald Kolsson, gathers skalds at royal court.

1152   Icelandic skald Einar Skulasson composes *The Ray of Light* in honour of St Olaf and recites it at Nidaros Cathedral, built over ruins of earlier church which housed St Olaf's remains.

Magnus V Erlingsson (1162–84)

            Magnus' maternal grandfather was Sigurd Jorsalfar; Magnus pledges Norway as a fief to the Church in return for its support of his claim to the throne; puts down uprisings of the *Birkebeiner* under Sverre, who claims to be the son of Sigurd Mund.

1170   'Historical' sagas begin and continue until *c.* 1250.

1184   Sverre kills Magnus at Battle of Nordnes.

Sverre Sigurdsson (1184–1202)

            Sverre draws support from small landowners (the *Birkebeiner* or 'Birch-legs') and defies the Church, whose prerogatives he diminishes; he founds a new commerce-based nobility.

1200   Icelandic 'family' sagas begin and continue to *c.* 1300.

Haakon III Sverresson (1202–4)
> Haakon dies young, probably poisoned.

Inge II Baardsson (1204–17)
> Placed in power by the Church, Inge is brother to Earl Skule, whom Sigrid Undset made the ancestor of Erlend Nikulausson.

Haakon IV Haakonsson the Lame (illegitimate son of Haakon III) (1217–63)
> Haakon, raised secretly by the *Birkebeiner*, is chosen king over Church objection. His rule ·brings Norway to its medieval zenith, with an end to the civil wars, great prosperity and the flowering of Old Norse literature.

c. 1220   Translation of the Bible into Norwegian is completed.

c. 1222   Snorri Sturluson writes the *Prose Edda.*

1223   Great Council at Bergen reaffirms Haakon's kingship.

1226   Haakon commissions Brother Robert to translate *Tristan and Iseut.*

1240   Earl Skule rebels and is slain by *Birkebeiners*; end of civil wars. Haakon is recognised by Pope Innocent IV.

1247   Haakon is crowned at Nidaros by the papal legate.

1263   Haakon falls in Battle of Largs.

Magnus VI Haakonsson the Law-Mender (1263–80)
1266   Magnus ends Scottish war and cedes Hebrides and Isle of Man to Alexander III.

c. 1270   Oldest known manuscript of the *Volsungasaga* is included in manuscript of the *Elder Edda.*

1274   Magnus promulgates new legal code accepting crime as offence against the state, not the individual.

1277   Magnus reaches agreement with Church about extent of its powers.

1280   At Magnus' death, the aristocracy is so weak it cannot dispute accession of Magnus' minor son Erik. *Njal's Saga* and other sagas are composed.

Erik Magnusson Priest-Hater (1280–99)

Haakon V Magnusson (1299–1319)
1299   Haakon declares Oslo his capital; around this time the

137

practice of saga writing ceases.

[Period of the *Master of Hestviken* begins about here.]

| 1308 | Haakon first weakens, then abolishes power of *lendermaend*; his daughter Lady Ingeborg marries Duke Erik of Sweden (later she marries Knut Porse). |

Magnus VII Eriksson (1319–43)

[The Black Death ravages Scandinavia from *c.* 1320 to *c.* 1380.]

| 1319 | Magnus accedes to thrones of Norway and Sweden at the age of three. |

[Period of *Kristin Lavransdatter* begins about here]

| 1332 | At Magnus' majority, Norwegian opposition to Swedish union and his neglect of Norway make Magnus recognise his son Haakon as his successor in Norway; development of prose folk literature forms the *eventyr* and the *sagn*. |

[Period of *The Master of Hestviken* ends about here.]

Haakon VI Magnusson (1343–80)
| 1356 | Magnus' son Erik revolts and claims part of Sweden, which Magnus regains at Erik's death in 1359. |

[Period of *Kristin Lavransdatter* ends about here.]

| 1363 | Hanseatic League establishes colony at Bergen, causing Norway to ally itself with Denmark through Haakon's marriage to Margarete, daughter of King Waldemar IV of Denmark; Magnus is deposed by Swedes and dies in Norway, *c.* 1373. |
| 1380 | Haakon dies. |

Olaf V Haakonsson (also King of Denmark) (1380–7)
| | Upon Olaf's death the Norwegian royal line is extinct, and throne is filled by election of Margarete, Olaf's mother. |

Margarete (1387–9)

Erik of Pomerania (Margarete's great nephew) (1387–97)
| 1397 | Erik is crowned King of Norway, Sweden and Denmark, in a union 'never to be dissolved': it lasts until the beginning of the nineteenth century. In the sixteenth century, Danish becomes Norway's written language. |

II. *The Nineteenth Century in Norway*

1814 *14 January*: Danish King Frederick VI cedes Norway to Sweden without consulting Norwegians.
17 May: (*Syttende Mai*) Norwegians frame Constitution and establish Storthing; two-week rebellion against Sweden.
4 November: Norway is declared a 'free, independent and indivisible kingdom' under Swedish king.

1818 Norwegian nobility is abolished.

1833 First 'Peasant Storthing' demands strict government economy.

c. 1850 Ivar Aasen develops *landsmål* (native form of the language known as *nynorsk*, linking peasant dialects and saga language to contemporary literature) to replace Dano-Norwegian *riksmål*; abolition of English Navigation Acts opens future for Norwegian merchant fleet.

1853 Ingvald Undset is born near Trondheim.

1857 Ibsen's *The Warriors at Helgeland* indicates rising interest in Norway's past, also shown in collections of Norwegian folk tales and ballads, dictionaries, and cultural histories by various authors.

1855 Camilla Collett publishes *The Governor's Daughters*, first realistic depiction of women's lives in modern Norway.

III. *Sigrid Undset's Life**

1871   Ingvald Undset matriculates at Cathedral School, Trondheim.

late   Ingvald Undset meets Anne Charlotte Gyth while attending
1870s   University of Copenhagen.

1880   Ingvald Undset marries Anne Charlotte Gyth.

1881   Undset's *The Beginnings of the Iron Age in Northern Europe* makes him an international reputation.

1882   20 May: **Sigrid Undset is born at Kalundborg, Denmark.**

1884   Undset family moves to Christiania (Oslo), near Vestre Aker Church.

1886   The Undsets move to 10 Lyder Sagens Street; Sigrid hears stories of Troy.

1888   Ingvald Undset makes research trip to Valdres with Mathiesen; works until 1892 on memoirs *From Akershus to the Acropolis*.

1890   Ingvald Undset writes *The First Beginnings of the Oslo Valley*. Sigrid meets Olaf at Drøbak that summer.

1891   The Undsets move to 5 Keysers Street.

1892   Family moves to Observatory Street, where Sigrid reads mythology and Old Norse texts with her father, as well as attending Ragna Nielson's Liberal school from 1892 to 1897.

1893   Sigrid read *Njal's Saga* at Trondheim in summer; her father dies in December.

1894   The family moves to Steen Street; Theodor Kittelson discourages Sigrid from pursuing career in art.

1897   Sigrid graduates from middle school.

---

* The information given here is adapted from unpaginated text preceding the Introduction to Carl Bayerschmidt, *Sigrid Undset* (New York: Twayne, 1970).

Literary and Historical Events

1871   Revised Act of Union with Sweden is defeated and Norwegian Venstre Party is founded. Heinrich Schliemann is excavating at Hissarlik, Turkey, site of ancient Troy.
In Norway there is a period of realism in drama and fiction, at its peak from 1870 to the late 1880s. Tension with Sweden increases during the last decades of the century.

1873   Norway celebrates 1,000 years as a kingdom.

1877   Ibsen writes *The Pillars of Society* and *A Doll's House*.
1879   Schliemann is excavating at Mycenae.

1881   From now until about 1910 Norwegians begin to emigrate to the USA in large numbers.
Henrik Ibsen's *Ghosts* shocks Norway and the world.

1884   Sverdrup is named Norwegian Prime Minister.

1886   Ibsen writes *Rosmersholm*.

1889   Sverdrup resigns; Ibsen writes *Hedda Gabler*.

1891   Ibsen returns to Norway after his self-imposed exile.

1898	Sigrid graduates from Olso's Commercial College.
1899	Sigrid begins ten years of employment with the German Electric Company in Oslo, during which she reads widely and begins to write.
1902	Sigrid Undset begins a novel set in the mid-thirteenth century. By 1905 it is completed but rejected by Gyldendal.
1907	*Fru Marta Oulie*, Sigrid Undset's first novel, is published.
1908	'The Happy Age' (short fiction, not trans.) and 'In the Grey Light of Dawn' (play, not trans.) published.
1909	*Gunnar's Daughter* is published. Sigrid receives study scholarship for travel; lives in Rome; meets Anders Castus Svarstad at Christmas.
1910	Returns to Oslo in the autumn and meets Nini Roll Anker; publishes 'Youth' (poems, not trans.).
1911	Writes the novel *Jenny* during the summer, which is published that autumn; it becomes the most widely-read novel in Norway that winter.
1912	Sigrid marries Anders C. Svarstad in Antwerp and they live in England. She publishes 'Some Reflections on the Suffragette Movement' and 'Poor Fortunes' (short stories, three of which are trans. in *Four Stories*); she and Svarstad move to Rome in December.
1913	12 January: Sigrid's first son Anders is born in Rome; in April she returns to Oslo with sickly child. In July, she takes up residence with Svarstad at Ski, near Oslo.
1914	Gives address, 'The Fourth Commandment', to Students' Union, Oslo; she also publishes 'Spring' (novel, not trans.).
1915	'Tales of King Arthur and the Knights of the Round Table' (not trans.) is published; daughter Maren Charlotte (Tulla) is born 29 October.
1916	Sigrid and her family move to East Aker district of Olso.
1917	Spends summer at Laurgaard, near Sel in the Gudbrandsdal.

142

1899	Norway's National Theatre is established; Ibsen writes his last play, *When We Dead Awaken*; Adolf Hitler is born.
1900	Norwegian legislation brings *riksmål* (*bokmål*), the national language, also called Dano-Norwegian, closer to *landsmål* (*nynorsk*), the country language or language of the people.
1905	Norway severs union with Sweden; Haakon VII crowned at Trondheim.
1906	Ibsen dies in Olso.
1907	Norwegian women receive limited voting rights.
1913	Norway becomes first sovereign country in Europe to extend full voting rights to women.
1914	The First World War begins in August; Norway remains neutral. Hitler enlists in Bavarian Army.
1917	In October the Bolshevik Revolution takes place in Russia, followed by Civil War.

1918	'The Wise Virgins' (of which only 'Thjodolf' is trans.) is published.
1919	Sigrid and her children move to Lillehammer in July; she is tacitly separated from Svarstad; her third child, Hans, is born in August. She publishes essays 'A Woman's Point of View' and 'Postscript to the Fourth Commandment'.
1920	Sigrid purchases Bjerkebaek at Lillehammer; *The Bridal Wreath* is published. The period 1921–13 is recorded in *Happy Times in Norway*.
1921	*The Mistress of Husaby* is published.
1922	*The Cross* is published.
1923	Sigrid's translation to modern Norwegian of 'Three Sagas of Icelanders' (not trans. to English) is published.
1924	On 23 November Sigrid's marriage to Svarstad is annulled; on 24 November she is received into Roman Catholic Church.
1925	Spends Easter at Monte Cassino with mother and son Anders. She publishes 'St Hallvard's Life, Death and Miracles' and *Olav Audunssøn i Hestviken* (trans. as *The Axe* and *The Snake Pit* of *The Master of Hestviken*).
1927	*Olav Audunssøn og Hans Børn* (trans. as *In the Wilderness* and *The Son Avenger* of *The Master of Hestviken*) published.
1928	Receives Nobel Prize for Literature and donates 15,000 Norwegian crowns to the Norwegian Authors' Association. 'Margaret Clitheroe' published.
1929	The essays *Stages on the Road*; the novel, *The Wild Orchid*; and the short work, 'And What If This Baby Were Not Born?' (not trans.) are published.
1930	*The Burning Bush*; 'Saint Olav, Norway's King' (not trans.), and 'The Christmas Miracle' (not trans.) are published.
1931	The essays 'Meeting and Parting' (*Begegnungen und Trennungen*) are published. *Sigurd and His Brave Companions* first appears, in German (*Die Saga von Vilmund Vidutan und seiner Gefährten*).
1932	*Ida Elisabeth* and 'Christmas and Twelfth Night' (not trans.) are published.
1933	More essays of *Stages on the Road* appear.

1918	11 November: Armistice ending the First World War is signed.
1919–1920	Peace settlements for the Russian Civil War are conducted. Hitler founds the NSDAP at Munich.
1923	8–9 November: Hitler's 'Beerhall Putsch' is put down by German Army in Munich; 1923–4 Hitler writes *Mein Kampf* in Landsberg Prison.
1924	Lenin dies and power struggle ensues in the USSR.
1927	Socialist (Labour) Party is dominant in Norwegian politics from this date.
1928	Stalin becomes victorious in the USSR and initiates first Five-Year Plan; collectivisation involves the liquidation of 5 million peasant households from 1928 to 1932.
1929	US Stock Market Crash in October is followed by Great Depression.
1931	Sino–Japanese War takes place.
1932	Nazis become largest (but not majority) party in Reichstag; Hitler loses election to von Hindenburg.
1933	Hindenburg appoints Hitler Chancellor of Germany; the Reichstag fire is blamed on the Communists and in March the Reichstag votes Hitler dictatorial powers.

1934	Sigrid's childhood autobiography *The Longest Years* and *Saga of Saints* are published.
1935	The essay 'Progress, Race, Religion' (not trans. to English) in direct reference to Nazi anti-Semitism is published. Sigrid attends meeting of Scandinavian authors in Helsinki.
1936	'The Faithful Wife' is published (not trans.); Sigrid's works are eliminated from German libraries.
1937	On 15 May the Norwegian Nazi newspaper *Fronten* denounces Sigrid Undset.
1938	The essays *Men, Women and Places* are published.
1939	Sigrid's last novel, *Madame Dorthea*, is published. In this year Sigrid's daughter Tulla and her mother die.
1940	6 April: Sigrid Undset gives address 'Christianity and Our Time' at Oslo Students' Union; 9 April: Nazis open invasion of Norway, 20 April: Sigrid flees from Lillehammer; 26 April: Anders dies with machine-gun unit, not far from Lillehammer; 8 June: Norway capitulates; 13 July: Sigrid leaves Sweden for Moscow, arriving at last in San Francisco 26 August. In Norway her books are destroyed by Nazis.
1941	Sigrid works and travels for Norwegian Information Service in the USA (until 1945); her articles this year include 'A Book That Was a Turning Point in My Life'.
1942	Sigrid writes *Happy Times in Norway* (trans. to Norwegian in 1947) and receives honorary doctorate from Rollins College; *Return to the Future* is published.
1943	*Sigurd and His Brave Companions* (orig. published in German, 1931) is published; Sigrid receives honorary doctorate from Smith College in May; July gives lecture 'Scandinavian Literature' to Polish Academy of Arts and Sciences in the United States.

1934	Nazis carry out blood purge of their party; they enact anti-semitic laws and set up concentration camps.
1935	Italy overwhelms Ethiopia.
1936	Hitler allies himself with Italy and remilitarises the Rhineland; Stalin carries out Great Purge in the USSR 1936–8; Spanish Civil War begins (ends 1939).
1938	March: Hitler annexes Austria; September: Britain and France sign Munich Pact, giving Czechoslovakia to Germany.
1939	23 August: Nazis sign mutual nonaggression pact with USSR. 1 September to 17 September: Nazis invade Poland in *Blitzkrieg*, opening 'phoney war', which lasts until the following spring. The USSR defeats Finland, 1939–40.
1940	May: British evacuate Dunkirk; 9 June: Italy enters war; 22 June: France capitulates; September: Battle of Britain; beginning of North African Campaign coincides with North Atlantic submarine warfare; October: Italy invades Greece.
1941	US Congress votes Lend-Lease aid to Britain; 6 April: Germany overcomes Greece and Yugoslavia; 22 June: Germany attacks USSR; August: Roosevelt and Churchill sign Atlantic Charter; 7 December Japanese attack on Pearl Harbor causes US declaration of war on 8 December: Nazi march on Moscow is halted by Soviet counter-offensive; Japan overruns Philippines, Malaya, Burma and Indonesia.
1942	7 August: US forces land on Guadalcanal in darkest period of the war for the Allies; Axis forces under Rommel sweep into Egypt and Nazis penetrate to the Caucasus, mounting offensive against Stalingrad. In October, Montgomery defeats Rommel at El Alamein, and on 8 November, US forces invade Algeria.
1943	2 February: German 6th Army surrenders at Stalingrad; 12 May: Africa is cleared of Axis forces; July and August: US occupation of Sicily; 8 September: Italy surrenders; end of Solomon Islands Campaign late in 1943.

147

1944	Sigrid writes on the Seventh Commandment for collection *The Ten Commandments*, striking out at Nazi activities in Norway.
1945	Sigrid edits and writes Introduction for *True and Untrue and Other Norse Tales* by Asbjørnsen and Moe; returns to Lillehammer in August; translates *Twelve Stories by Steen Blicher* from the Danish.
1946	Sigrid publishes articles on postwar situation: 'This is No Time for Pollyannas' (not trans.) and 'On Abraham's Sacrifice' (not trans.).
1947	Sigrid writes biography of St Catherine of Siena, rejected by Doubleday and not published until 1951 in Norwegian. 20 May: on Sigrid Undset's sixty-fifth birthday, King Haakon awards her the Grand Cross of the Order of St Olaf for service to Norway.
1948	Sigrid writes 'The Religion of Brotherhood' (not trans.).
1949	10 June: **Sigrid Undset dies at Lillehammer**. She is buried nearby at Mesnalien with Anders and Tulla.
1952	Sigrid's *Artikler og taler fra krigstiden* (not trans.; 'Articles and Tales from Wartime') is published, edited by A.H. Winsnes.
1954	*Catherine of Siena* is published in English.
1955	*Four Stories* is published by Knopf in Naomi Walford's translation.

1944	Rome falls to Allies after Battles of Anzio and Monte Cassino; submarine threat in North Atlantic is virtually ended; 6 June: Normandy Invasion is mounted; 15 August: Allied landing made in southern France; by October most of France and Belgium are liberated; Battle of the Bulge takes place in December.
1945	7 March: Allies cross the Rhine; 25 April: Western and Soviet Armies meet in Saxony; ? 30 April: Hitler commits suicide; 7 May: Germany surrenders unconditionally; 6 and 9 August: US drops atomic bombs on Japan; 14 August: Japan surrenders unconditionally.
1946	During postwar cold war period, Truman Doctrine halts Communist encroachments in Greece and Turkey and the Marshall Plan assists European economic recovery.
1948	The USSR blockades Berlin and the Western democracies institute the Berlin Airlift.
1949	The North Atlantic Treaty is signed, establishing NATO.
1950	North Korea attacks South Korea, beginning Korean Conflict.
1955	Warsaw Treaty Organisation is formed.

Bibliographical Notes

The authoritative primary sources of Sigrid Undset's fiction are *Middelalderromaner*, 10 vols. (Oslo: Aschehoug, 1956), and *Romaner og Fortellinger fra Nutiden*, 10 vols. (Oslo: Aschehoug, 1964). English translations of her work currently in print are the Bantam paperback editions of *Kristin Lavransdatter*: *The Bridal Wreath*, originally published by Knopf in 1920, translated by Charles Archer and J.S. Scott (New York: Bantam, 1978); *The Mistress of Husaby*, 1921, translated by Charles Archer (New York: Bantam, 1978); and *The Cross*, 1922, translated by Charles Archer (New York: Bantam, 1979). All three translations are available in collected form from Random House (New York, 1987) and as a Picador Classic (London: Pan, 1988). Also available is the 1978 collected New ʻAmerican Library Plume edition of *The Master of Hestviken* (*The Axe*, 1925; *The Snake Pit*, 1925; *In the Wilderness*, 1927; and *The Son Avenger*, 1927) translated by Arthur G. Chater (New York: Knopf, 1928, 1929 and 1930 respectively for individual volumes).

Besides W. Emmé's 1921 translation of *Jenny*, originally published in 1911, Knopf also published English translations by Arthur G. Chater of the rest of Sigrid Undset's novels: *The Wild Orchid*, 1929, trans. 1931; *The Burning Bush*, 1930, trans. 1933; *Ida Elisabeth*, 1932, trans. 1933; *Gunnar's Daughter*, 1909, trans. 1933; *The Faithful Wife*, 1936, trans. 1937; and *Madame Dorthea*, 1939, trans. 1940. Translations of Sigrid Undset's short fiction appear in *Images in a Mirror*, 1917, translated by Arthur G. Chater (New York: Knopf, 1938), which contains 'Mrs Hjelde' and *Four Stories*, translated by Naomi Walford (New York: Knopf, 1959), containing 'Selma Brøter', 'Miss Smith-Tellefsen' 'Simonsen', all originally published in 1912, and 'Thjodolf', originally published in 1918.

Essay collections by Sigrid Undset, both translated by Chater and published by Knopf, are *Stages on the Road*, 1933, trans. 1934; and *Men, Women and Places*, 1938, trans. 1939. E.C. Ramsden translated *Saga of Saints*, 1934, for Knopf in 1934. For children, Sigrid Undset also wrote *Sigurd and His Brave Companions* (New

York: Knopf, 1943), originally in German, and translated into Norwegian in 1955 by Signe Undset Thomas. Sigrid Undset edited and compiled *True and Untrue and Other Stories* (New York: Knopf, 1945), a translation of the Asbjørnson–Moe folk tale collection.

Although Sigrid Undset never wrote a complete autobiography, Knopf published Chater's translation of her 1934 childhood memoir, *The Longest Years*, in 1935 (a reprint is now available from Kraus Reprints, Millwood, New York); *Return to the Future*, Sigrid Undset's account of her flight from Norway in 1941, in Henriette C.K. Naeseth's translation, 1942; and Sigrid Undset's 1942 memoir for children, *Happy Times in Norway*, translated by Joran Birkeland, 1942. Sigrid Undset also provided a brief but revealing autobiographical sketch for *Twentieth Century Authors*, edited by Stanley J. Kunitz and Howard Haycroft (New York: H.W. Wilson, 1942; 7th printing 1973), pp. 1,431–5.

Translated works are cited by their English titles. Untranslated works are cited by translations of their original titles, indicated by quotation marks. Except for a few short translations identified in the footnotes, passages otherwise inaccessible to English-speaking readers have been cited from the only two full-length studies of Sigrid Undset's life and works currently available in English. A.H. Winsnes was able to consult with Sigrid Undset herself shortly before her death for *Sigrid Undset: A Study in Christian Realism*, originally published by Aschehoug in 1949 and translated by P.G. Foote (New York: Sheed and Ward, 1953). Carl Bayerschmidt's *Sigrid Undset* (New York: Twayne, 1970), follows Winsnes closely in biographical matters, but Bayerschmidt offers fresh interpretations of several of Sigrid Undset's works. For readers of Norwegian, Charlotte Blindheim's *Moster Sigrid. Et familie portrett av Sigrid Undset* (Olso: Aschehoug, 1982) is a graceful personal memoir translated in part in *The Scandinavian Review* vol. 70, no. 2 (June 1982), pp. 39–54. Borghild Krane's *Sigrid Undset. Liv og meninger* (Oslo: Gyldendal, 1970), which is not available in English, was written from the experience of an association with Sigrid Undset in her last years. The Norwegian Information Service in the United States commissioned several otherwise unpublished essays in English by her friends and critics for the 1982 centennial of Sigrid Undset's birth: 'Russia — and Sigrid Undset', by Katarina Enokovna Muradjan; 'Sigrid Undset

Seen Through the Eyes of an American Woman Religious', by Margaret Mary Dunn; 'Sigrid Undset: The Nobel Prize Laureate who Loved Brooklyn Bridge', by Arne Skouen; 'Sigrid Undset — 1882–1982', by Hallvard Rieber-Mohn; 'Sigrid Undset: Woman's Place', by Kirsten Wisloff Andresen; 'Sigrid Undset and Germany', by Heiko Uecker; and 'For Sigrid Undset', by Regis Boyer.

Useful short critical studies are Harald Beyer's 'Sigrid Undset', in *A History of Norwegian Literature*, translated and edited by Einar Haugen (New York: New York University Press, 1956), stressing Sigrid Undset's place in the tradition of Scandinavian realism; Alrik Gustafson's 'Christian Ethics in a Pagan World: Sigrid Undset', in *Six Scandinavian Novelists* (Minneapolis: University of Minnesota Press, 1968), critical of Sigrid Undset's dogmatic neothomism but fair in its assessment of her literary position; and my own overview essay, 'Sigrid Undset', in *A Critical Study of Long Fiction* (La Canada, California: Salem Press, 1983).

The following sources helpfully illuminate Sigrid Undset's 'two thousand years in Norway'. Two especially important studies of Old Norse mythology are Hilda R. Ellis Davidson's *Gods and Myths of Northern Europe* (Harmondsworth and New York: Penguin, 1964) and Georges Dumézil's *Gods of the Ancient Northmen*, edited by Einar Haugen and translated by C. Scot Littleton et al. (Berkeley, Calif.: University of California Press, 1974). Bertil Almgren's edition of *The Viking*, translated by T.R. Nicholson (New York: Crescent Books, 1980), contains handsome colour photographs and line drawings of Viking life as well as of archaeological discoveries; Charlotte Blindheim, as Curator of the Museum of National Antiquities of the University of Oslo, is one of its contributors. James Graham-Campbell's *The Viking World* (New York: Ticknor and Fields, 1980) also is a fine illustrated text. Gwyn Jones' *A History of the Vikings* (Oxford and New York: Oxford University Press, 1968) is a scholarly treatment of the historical period. Reliable discussions of the Icelandic sagas appear in Theodore M. Andersson's *The Icelandic Family Saga: An Analytic Reading* (Cambridge, Mass.: Harvard University Press, 1957); Carol J. Glover's *The Medieval Sagas* (Ithaca, N.Y.: Cornell University Press, 1982); and Peter Hallberg's *The Icelandic Saga*, translated by Paul Schach (Lincoln, Nebraska: University of Nebraska Press, 1962). Carl F. Bayerschmidt and Lee M. Hollander published the definitive English translation of *Njal's Saga* (London and Westport, Conn.: Greenwood Press, 1979 [1956]). Magnus Magnusson and Herman Palsson's translation is also available as a Penguin Classic (Harmondsworth and New York: Penguin, 1964). Jean I. Young's translation of Snorri Sturluson's *Prose Edda* (Berkeley, Calif.: University of California Press, 1954), remains the standard English version of this vital work, which is also available in a translation by A. Faulkes, published by Dent in the Everyman Classics series in 1987 (paperback).

Index

Works by Sigrid Undset

Titles of untranslated works are given in the original.

Artikler og taler fra krigstiden, 148
Axe, The, 84–6, 144

Begegnungen und Trennungen, 102, 112–13
'Blasphemy', 107
'Book That Was a Turning Point in My Life, A', 40, 146
Bridal Wreath, The, 67, 68–71, 144
Burning Bush, The, 100–2, 105, 107, 112

Catholic Propaganda, 93, 113
'Cavalier', 107
'Children of Ara Coeli', 43
'Christentum und Neuheidentum', 113
'Christianity and Our Time', 146
'Christmas and Twelfth Night', 144
Cross, The, 67, 73–5, 144

'D.H. Lawrence', 108–9
'Dream, A', 38, 39

Faithful Wife, The, 104–5, 146
Fattige skjebner, 47, 49, 52, 142
Fortellinger om Kong Arthur og ridderne av det runde bord, 142
'Fortschritt, Rasse, Religion', 114
Four Stories, 50–2, 142, 148
'Fourth Commandment, The', 54, 62, 142
Fru Marta Oulie, 20, 36, 37–8, 142
'Fru Waage', 58

Gefahrdung des Christentums durch Rassenwahn und Judenverfolgung, Die, 114
'Glastonbury', 108
Gunnar's Daughter, 40–2, 66, 142
Gunnvald og Emma, 60

'Half-Dozen Handkerchiefs, A', 38, 39
'Happy Age, The' (collection), *see, lykkeliger alder, Den*
'Happy Age, The' (short story), 35, 39, 40, 58
Happy Times in Norway, 80, 121, 144, 146
'Hellig Olav, Norges kong', 102, 144

Ida Elisabeth, 103–4, 144
In the Grey Light of Dawn, 38, 142
In the Wilderness, 84, 88–90, 144
'Inheritance Which Must Be Accepted, The', 93

Jenny, 44, 45–6, 142

kloge jomfruer, De, 59
Kristin Lavransdatter, 1, 2, 13, 64–79, 83, 125, 128, 129, 130, 131, 138
   see also Bridal Wreath, The; Mistress of Husaby, The; Cross, The

'Letter to a Parish Priest', 103, 113
Longest Years, The, 18–32, 97, 101–2, 146
'Lutheran Spirit and the Catholic Church, The', 93
lykkelige alder, Den, 38–40, 142

Madame Dorthea, 2, 20, 109–10, 146
'Margaret Clitheroe', 102, 144
Master of Hestviken, The, 1, 10, 36, 40, 80–94, 98, 125, 128, 129, 130, 131, 138, 144
   see also Axe, The; Snake Pit, The; In the Wilderness; Son Avenger, The
'Meetings and Partings', *see Begegnungen und Trennungen*
Men, Women and Places, 107, 146
'Miss Smith-Tellefsen', 51
Mistress of Husaby, The, 67, 71–3, 144
'Mrs Hjelde', 40, 58–9

'Olaf der Heilige. Christentum und germanisches Naturheidentum', 113
'Om folkviser', 67
'On Abraham's Sacrifice', 122, 148
'On Ballads' *see* 'Om folkviser'

155

'Poor Fortunes', *see Fattige skjebner*
'Postscript to the Fourth
  Commandment', 144

Return to the Future, 115, 116–21, 146
'Robert Southwell, S.J.', 102
'Rückkehr zur katholischen Kirche',
  113

*Saga von Vilmund Vidutan und seiner
  Gefährten, Die*, 121, 144, 146
Saga of Saints, 7–8, 11, 73, 105–7,
  146
'St. Hallvard's Life, Death and
  Miracles', 144
'Scandinavian Literature', 126, 146
'Selma Brøter', 50
*Sigurd and His Brave Companions, see
  Saga von Vilmund Vidutan und seiner
  Gefährten, Die*
'Simonsen', 51–2
'Smaapiker', 60
Snake Pit, The, 84–8, 144
'Some Reflections on the Suffragette
  Movement', 52, 142
Son Avenger, The, 84, 90–3, 144
Splinten av roldspeilet, 58–9
'Spring', *see Vaaren*
Stages on the Road, 102–4, 144
*Stories and Legends of Holy Men and
  Women*, 36

'Stranger, A', 38, 39
'Strongest Power, The', 107, 108
'Summer in Gotland', 108

'Tales of King Arthur and the
  Knights of the Round Table', *see
  Fortellinger om Kong Arthur og ridderne
  av det runde bord*
'This is No Time for Polyannas', 148
'Thjodolf', 60, 144
'Three Sagas of Icelanders', 144
True and Untrue and Other Norse Tales,
  121, 148
  see also Asbjørnson–Moe,
  'Norwegian Folk Tales' (General)

Ungdom, 40, 142

Vaaren, 20, 55–6, 129, 142

Weihnachtswunder, Das, 102, 112, 144
'What Catholicism Thinks of Luther',
  93
Wild Orchid, The, 98, 99–100, 112,
  144
'Woman's Point of View, A', 60, 61,
  144
'Women and the World War', 62

Yearling, The, 121
'Youth', *see Ungdom*

General

Aanrud, Hans, 122
Aasen, Ivar, 14, 139
Act of Union, 13
  Revised, 15, 141
Adrian IV, Pope, *see*, Breakspear,
  Nicholas
Aeschylus, *The Agamemnon*, 25
Aesir, 5, 6
Aethelbert, 4
Aethelstan, 9
Age of Reason, The, 109
Age of Sagas, 9, 135–7
Alexander III, 12, 137
Allen, Hope Emily, 121
Althing, 8
Anker, Nini Roll, 16 *n*2, 42, 44, 46,
  49, 53, 57, 61, 78 *n*10, 142
  *Min venn Sigrid
  Undset*, 43
  The Weaker Sex, 42
Aquinas, St Thomas, 98
Arnold, Matthew, 97
Arthur, 4, 133
Asbjørnson–Moe, 'Norwegian Folk

Tales', 14, 148
Asgard, 5, 6
Attila the Hun, 3, 133

Bagler, 10
Baldwin, I, 136
Barrés, Maurice, 97
Beowulf, 4, 133
berserker, 11, 85, 97, 131
billedteppe, 59, 63 *n*8
Birkebeiner, 10, 71, 83, 136, 137
Bjørnson, Bjørnstjerne, 14, 15, 34, 66
Black Death, The, 13, 68, 138
Blicher, Steen Steensen
  Birds of Passage, 20
  Twelve Stories by Steen Blicher, 148
Blindheim, Charlotte, 34, 35, 57, 64,
  80, 115, 117, 121, 123, 128, 129
Blundell, William, 107
bokmål, see riksmål
bönder, 106
Brandes, Georg, 35, 52
  William Shakespeare, 35
Breakspear, Nicholas, 10, 65, 136

Bregendahl, Marie, 108
Brontë, Emily, 'The Prisoner', 35
Brown, George Mackay, 7
Bourget, Paul, 97
Bull, Edvard, *Nation and Church in the Middle Ages*, 67
Byrhtnoth, 134

Carl XIV, 13
Carl XV, 15
Cather, Willa, 121
Catherine of Siena, 122, 148
Catholic Renewal Movement, 97
Chartist Movement, 52
Chater, Arthur, 21
Chesterton, G.K., 97
Christian IV, 34
Claudel, Paul, 2, 97
Collett, Camilla, 15, 127, 139
    The Governor's Daughters, 15, 139
Cromwell, Oliver, 107

Daae and Drolsum, *The History of the World*, 28, 35
Davidson, Hilda Ellis, 7, 76
Day, Dorothy, 121
Dickens, Charles, 35
Diplomatarium Norvegicum, 67
Dumézil, Georges, 5
Dunn, Margaret Mary, 122

Eddas, 6, 7
    see also *Elder Edda, The*; and *Younger (Prose) Edda, The*
Egil Skalla-Grimsson, 9
Einar Skulasson, *The Ray of Light*, 136
Einstein, Albert, *The Theory of Relativity*, 96
Elder Edda, The, 4, 5, 137
Eliot, T.S., 97, 131
English Civil War, 107
Enlightenment, The, 20
Erik, Duke of Sweden, 12, 68, 138
Erik of Pomerania, 13, 138
Erik Bloodaxe, 8, 9, 133–4
Erik Haakonsson, 134
Erik Magnusson Priest-hater, 9, 83, 137
Erling Vidkunsson, 68
eventyr, 12, 14
Eystein, Saint, 106
Eystein I Magnusson, 136
Eystein II, 136

Fagstad, Helene, 43, 45
Fascism, 96, 104
Fielding, Henry, 35
First World War, 52, 54, 57, 119, 126, 143, 145

Forsberg, Dea, 36
Frederick VI, 139
Frederick VIII, 15
Freud, Sigmund, 26, 95
    Three Essays on the Theory of Sexuality, 95
Freyja, 3, 6, 76, 77, 131
Freyr (Yng), 3, 5, 6, 21, 76
Frigg, 77
Fronten, 114, 146
futhark, 9
fylker, 4

German Electric Company, 33, 142
German Romantic Movement, 66, 127
gothar, 8
Grand Cross of the Order of Saint Olaf, 122, 148
Gundiharius, 3
Gyth, Anne Charlotte, *see* Undset, Anne Charlotte Gyth

Haakon I Haroldsson the Good, 9, 134
Haakon II Sigurdsson, 9, 134
Haakon III Sverresson, 137
Haakon IV Haakonsson the Lame, 10, 11, 127, 137
Haakon V Magnusson, 34, 68, 69, 137
Haakon VI Magnusson, 83, 138
Haakon VII, 15, 143
Halfdan the Black, 7, 133
Hallvard, Saint, 106
Hamsun, Knut, 7
Hanseatic League, 12, 68, 138
Harold Fairhair, 7, 8, 10, 11, 133–4, 136
Harold II Eriksson Greycloak, 134
Harold III Haardrade, 135
Harold Gille (Gilchrist), 136
Harold Godwinson, 135
Hávamál, 5, 90, 125
Heiberg, Gunnar, 34, 36, 37, 38
    The People's Council, 36
    The Tragedy of Love, 36, 38
Heimskringla, 11, 105
von Hindenburg, Paul, 145
Hitler, Adolf, 3, 96, 101, 107, 109, 112, 113, 117, 127, 143, 145, 147, 149
    Mein Kampf, 96, 145
Holberg, Ludwig, 25, 28
Huxley, Aldous, 97

Ibsen, Henrik, 7, 14, 34, 37, 75, 139, 141, 143
    A Doll's House, 37, 141

Ghosts, 141
Hedda Gabler, 37, 141
The Pillars of Society, 141
Rosmersholm, 141
The Warriors at Helgeland, 139
When We Dead Awaken, 143
The Wild Duck, 34
Inge (King of Sweden), 135
Inge I, 136
Inge II Baardsson, 10, 137
Ingeborg (also Lady Ingebjørg), 12, 68, 72, 138

Keats, John, 35
Kempe, Margery, 108
Kiel, Treaty of, 13
Kittelson, Theodor, 33, 140
Knut the Great, 135
Knut Porse, 68, 138
Kures, Anne, 55

Lady Ingebjørg, *see* Ingeborg
Lagerkvist, Per, 7
landsmål, 1, 14, 30, 139, 143
Landsted, M.B., *Norwegian Ballads*, 14
Lawrence, D.H., 7, 18, 68, 131
Legends and Tales of Antiquity, 27
Leif Eriksson, 134
lendermaend, 12, 83, 134, 138
Lenin, Vladimir Ilych, 145
Lie, Jonas, 34, 127
Loki, 5
Lull, Ramon, 103
Luther, Martin, 112
Lutz, A.J., O.P., 98

Magnus, Saint, 106
Magnus I Olafsson the Good, 9, 135
Magnus II Haroldsson, 135
Magnus III Olafsson the Barefoot, 135
Magnus IV Sigurdsson, 136
Magnus V, 10
Magnus VI Law-mender, 10, 11, 12, 56, 68, 69, 83, 137
Magnus VII Eriksson, 12, 68, 72, 138
Malamud, Bernard, 97
Maldon, Battle of, 57, 134
Malory, Sir Thomas, *Le Morte Darthur*, 56
Mann, Thomas, 107, 121, 131
The Magic Mountain, 107
Margarete, 138
Maritain, Jacques, 2, 98, 121
Martha, Crown Princess, 122
Marxism, 114
Mathiesen, Henrik, 18, 24, 30, 140
Mauriac, François, 97
Merici, Angela, 103

Moe, Ragna, 43, 57
Møller, Kitti Anker, *A Birth Policy for Women*, 61–2
Mosse, *see* Tulla
Munan Baardsson, 83
Munich Pact, 147

Nansen, Peter, 36
Naturalism, 14
Navigation Acts, 14, 139
Nazism, 96, 105, 109, 110, 112, 113, 114, 115, 116, 118, 119, 120, 147
Neothomism, 98, 99, 100
Nielsen, Ragna, 27, 31, 43, 140
Njal's Saga, 11, 29, 36, 40, 61, 116, 128, 140
Njála, see *Njal's Saga*
Nobel Prize for Literature, 1, 94, 95, 115, 121, 122, 144
Norns, The, 5
Norske Folkeventyr, see Asbjørnson–Moe, 'Norwegian Folk Tales'
Norske Folkevisor, see Landsted, M.G., *Norwegian Ballads*
Norwegian Authors' Guild, 115
Norwegian Information Service, 119, 146
Norwegian National Movement, 13–16
Norwegian National Romanticism, 14
Norwegian Resistance, 119
Norwegian Socialist (Labour) Party, 145
Novalis (Friedrich von Hardenberg), 66, 127
nynorsk, see *landsmål*

Odin (also Wotan, Woden), 3, 4, 5, 6, 8, 11, 29, 76, 77, 81, 84, 85, 90, 110, 131
Olaf I Tryggvasson, 4, 6, 9, 42, 66, 105, 134
Olaf II Haroldsson the Fat (Saint Olaf), 9, 106, 127, 135, 136
Olaf III Haroldsson the Quiet, 135
Olaf IV Magnusson, 136
Olaf V Haakonsson, 138
Old Norse mythology, 4–8, 9, 29
Oscar II, 15

Paasche, Fredrik, 16, 67
Pankhurst, Emmeline, 52
positivism, 14
Prose Edda, see Younger Edda

Ragnarok, 5
Ragnvald Kolsson, 136
Rawlings, Marjorie Kinnan, 121

The Yearling, 121
Revised Act of Union, see Act of
Union
riksmål, 14, 139, 143
Rilke, Rainer Maria, 125, 131
Roosevelt, Eleanor, 80
Roosevelt, Franklin Delano, 119
Ruskin, John, 97
Russian Civil War, 143, 145

Sagas, 30, 67, 135–6
sagn, 12
Sandvig, Anders, 65
Saxo Grammaticus, *Gesta Danorum*, 5
Schelling, Father Karl, 106
Schliemann, Heinrich, 18, 22, 141
Scholasticism, see Thomism
Second Vatican Council, 125
Second World War, 115–23, 130,
147–9
Seymour-Smith, Martin, 95
Shelley, Percy Bysshe, 35
Sif, 81, 84
Sigurd I Magnusson Jorsalfar, 105,
136
Sigurd II Haroldsson Mund, 136
Sigvat Thórdarsson, 9
Sino-Japanese War, 145
skalds, 4, 8, 9, 134–5
Skouen, Arne, 119, 121
Skram, Amalie, 14, 34, 127
Skule, 10, 11, 83, 137
Snorri Sturluson, 11, 105, 126, 137
Meimskringla, 11, 105
Southwell, Robert, 102
'The Burning Babe', 102
Stalin, Josef, 109, 117, 144, 147
Storthing, 13, 15, 36, 139
Strindberg, August, 7
Stromsted, Mrs Alf Jorgen, 121, 125
Styron, William, 97
Suffragette Movement, 52–3
Sunniva, Saint, 106
Svarstad, Anders, 53, 55, 57, 81,
116–17, 121, 123, 126, 142, 146,
148
Svarstad, Anders Castus, 43, 44, 47,
49, 53, 55, 57, 60, 61, 62, 73, 78,
79 n10, 142, 144
'Factory Girl', 44
'Myren's Workshop in Oslo, 1903',
44
Svarstad, Ebba, 81
Svarstad, Hans, 57, 62, 81, 109, 117,
118, 122, 144
Svarstad, Maren Charlotte, *see* Tulla
Svein Haakonsson, 134–5
Svein Knutsson, 135
Sverdrup, Johan, 15, 26, 141

Sverre Sigurdsson, 10, 136
Syttende Mai (17 May), 13, 80, 139

Tacitus, *Germania*, 4, 133
Ten Commandments, The, 148
Theodoric, 3
Thomas of Britain, 10
Tristan and Iseut, 10, 137
Thomas, Signe Undset, 122
Thomism, 98, 101
Thor, 3, 5, 6, 8, 76, 77, 81, 84, 105,
131
Thorfinn, Saint, 106
Tristan and Iseut, see Thomas of Britain
Tuchman, Barbara, 93
Tulla (Maren Charlotte Svarstad;
'Mosse'), 57, 81, 116, 118 123, 126,
142, 146, 148

Uecker, Heiko, 114
Undset, Anne Charlotte Gyth, 19, 20,
21, 24, 26, 27, 28, 30, 31, 56, 109,
140, 146
Undset, Ingvald, 18, 19, 22, 23, 24,
26, 27, 30, 31, 32, 34, 67, 71, 139,
140
From Akershus to the Acropolis, 24,
140
*The Beginnings of the Iron Age in
Northern Europe*, 19, 140
*The First Beginnings of the Oslo
Valley*, 24, 240
Undset, Sigrid
antagonism to Germans, 22, 43, 93,
112, 117, 120
appearance in late twenties, 43
attacks on Nazism, 2, 114, 117,
119–21
attitude to art, 125–6
childhood, 18–32
conversion, 2, 78, 82
devotion to Old Norse past, 1, 2,
7–8, 16, 22, 25, 28–9, 40, 67,
76–7, 105–7, 126ff., 128, 131
dislike of school, 27–8, 31
exile in United States, 115–21
in Scandinavian realistic tradition,
7, 52, 125–6
love of literature, 28–9, 34–5
love of sketching, 30, 33
Nobel Prize, 94–5, 115
postwar grief, 122
relationship with children, 57, 81ff,
116–17
relationship with father, 21–32
relationship with mother, 19–20
relationship with Svarstad, 43ff.,
53–4, 62, 78–9
religious views, 2, 22–3, 28, 30, 31,

54, 59, 61, 93, 95, 97–8, 102ff.,
107–8
views on feminism, 37, 46–7, 50,
52–3, 61–2
views on maternity, 110
views on sexuality, 25, 45–6,
128–9
Ungar, *Stories and Legends of Holy Men and Women*, 36

Vanir, 5, 6
Venstre ('Left') Party, 15, 141
Viking Age, the, 8, 9, 127, 133–5
Vikings, 1, 4, 12, 22, 57, 66, 81, 84,
106, 120
Volsungasaga, The, 8, 86, 133, 137
Voluspå, The, 134

Waldemar IV, 138

Waugh, Evelyn, 97
Webster, John, 49
Weismantel, Leo, 108
Welhaven, Johan Sebastian, 14
Well of Mimir, 5, 6
Wergeland, Henrik, 13, 15
wergild, 12, 83
Westdeutscher Beobachter, 114
World War I, *see* First World War
World War II, *see* Second World War
Wotan (also Woden), *see* Odin

Yggdrasil, 5
Yng, *see* Freyr
Younger (Prose) Edda, 4, 5, 11, 105,
137

Zola, Emile, 14, 52